THE OLD-FASHIONED
CUTTING GARDEN

THE
OLD-FASHIONED
CUTTING GARDEN

Growing Flowers
for Pleasure and Profit

JACK KRAMER

Drawings by Judifer Yellich

MACMILLAN PUBLISHING CO., INC.

NEW YORK

Macmillan Publishing Co., Inc.
866 Third Avenue, New York, N.Y. 10022
Collier Macmillan Canada, Ltd.

Library of Congress Cataloging in Publication Data
Kramer, Jack, 1927–
The old-fashioned cutting garden.
Includes index.
1. Flower gardening. 2. Flowers. I. Title.
SB405.K7   635.9   78-21918
ISBN 0-02-566620-7

Designed by Philip Grushkin

First Printing 1979

Printed in the United States of America

CONTENTS

FLOWERS TO YOU!

IF YOU HAVE BOUGHT cut flowers—even a dozen daisies—for indoor bouquets or colorful accents, for a special party, or just to cheer up yourself, you know how expensive this indulgence can be. It doesn't have to be, though. You can grow your own flowers—lovely cosmos, lofty lupines, and a variety of other colorful blooms to decorate your home and lift your spirits as well. There are few secrets to growing flowers; with just some basic information you can grow cut flowers in the smallest of sites.

We now know the advantage of growing our own food (no matter how little the site). Flavor is better and cost is minimal compared to what you pay in stores. In the same way, you can grow flowers (and lots of them) in little space, if you know what you are doing.

With only a dozen kinds of flowers you can keep your house colorful almost all year and have ready blossoms for those special occasions, or not so special, when you just want a few flowers to brighten your day.

Good flower-gardening depends on good soil, ample water, and proper selection of plants, and we tell you how to do it. We discuss familiar cut flowers and not-so-familiar ones that you might want to grow, and tell you where to grow your productive garden, whether you have a large or small site. Also included are how to start your own flowers from seed, how to arrange and cut flowers, and how to harvest them. This book is for anyone who wants colorful blooms as part of their daily living. You can grow flowers easily and keep beauty around you on a shoestring budget.

So, whether to gain pleasure or save money by growing your own, you can have beautiful flowers indoors almost all year round with this book in hand.

J J K

THE OLD-FASHIONED
CUTTING GARDEN

I

Your Flower Garden

THERE ARE many kinds of gardens you can have on your property, no matter how small the space: vegetable, herb, foliage; but it is the flower garden that in the long run will prove the most rewarding. Besides furnishing you with delightful color outdoors, the flower garden provides you with exquisite cut flowers for the home. Whether for table centerpieces or for refreshing color accents, cut flowers are welcome additions to your everyday living, especially during the cold winter months when your spirits need a lift.

Decades ago the flower garden was as common as a coffee pot in the kitchen. Today I think we need a return of this little old-fashioned beauty, and the cutting garden definitely provides this welcome gift. It is a nice piece of yesterday for today, and, as it was in the past, it is beautiful and functional. And it saves money.

PLANTING
THE FLOWER GARDEN

If you want your plants to produce flowers, you have to prepare the soil properly. I discuss soil more fully in Chapter 4, but for now it is necessary to mention that the soil must be prepared in advance; that is, you must spade, dig, turn over the soil, and then add nutrients to it so that the soil is porous and able to sustain plants. (This can be hard work if you try to tackle the whole plot all at once, but not if you do a little at a time.) The nutrients that you have to add to the existing soil can be compost, fresh soil, or a combination of both; some seasoned manure should also be added.

Note that this initial preparation is going to be somewhat expensive because you have to buy new soil, manure, and possibly a spade and/or pitchfork. You can try to use your existing soil, but chances are it is already spent of its nutrients because it has been gardened continually, maybe for many years. If you want to be sure of having full-sized, profuse blooms, you are going to have to spend some money, rather as if you were preparing for the arrival of a new baby.

At first you will be puzzled as to how much of this and how much of that to add. But this is not a big question. For example, if your garden is 10 × 20 feet, add *at least* one truckload of soil (6 cubic yards), *at least* 6 to 8 bushels of compost, and 1 or 2 bushels of rotted manure.

After you have added the nutrients to the soil, get out your shovel and dig in the nutrients. Mix the soil as you would mix a cake batter. Get the new into the old soil to recondition the soil properly. Turn and space and keep digging in until the soil is rich and black and smells woodsy.

If you have prepared a good nutritional soil, you can just pop plants in place and water them; they will almost grow by themselves. The proper soil and water are the main ingredients (along with sun) that will produce fragrant and lovely flowers for you.

WHAT TO GROW

This book is about cutting gardens, so you want flowers that grow easily, can be cut, and can be made into handsome displays for the house. Excellent cut flowers (and some dried flowers) can be taken from hundreds of annuals and perennials and some bulbs. There are flowers for everyone, and of course what you select depends upon your personal taste. None of the flowers listed and described in Chapter 5 is difficult to grow, and most respond beautifully to minimum care. However, if you are a beginning gardener, I recommend the following plants to get your cutting garden started:

Alyssum

Aster, China

Baby's Breath

Bachelor's Button

Blanketflower

Calendula

Candytuft

Chrysanthemum

Day Lily

Delphinium

Dianthus

Hollyhock

Marigold

Nasturtium

Phlox

Snapdragon

Summer Phlox

Zinnia

WHAT TO KNOW

To grow flowers properly you have to know the basic facts about soil, watering, feeding, insect protection and prevention, and culture. As we mentioned in the opening section, a rich porous soil is necessary for plants so that water can travel through the soil and thus reach the plant roots. Water heavily enough so that moisture drains into the soil to a good depth—at least 12 to 16 inches. It is better to water deeply and thoroughly a few times a week than to apply only a little at a time every day. Indeed, this underwatering could kill the plants.

You also have to feed plants occasionally, but this should

be done with a judicious hand. Too much feeding can kill plants, and not enough food may hinder growth. So know the dozens of plant foods—consult Chapter 4 for a detailed discussion of many of the fertilizers. And you have to learn a little about pesty insects because the more you know about them, the easier it will be to combat them *without* using expensive spraying materials and equipment. If you know the insect you are fighting before you do battle, any infestation can be remedied if caught early.

I am not discussing sunlight extensively because either you have it or you don't. Most flowers need sun, at least four hours a day, and if they do not get it, you cannot expect a bountiful harvest. However, some plants, such as impatiens and salvia, can grow in a somewhat shady place. So if your garden is shady, select plants which can tolerate this condition. The quick-reference charts at the end of the book include sunlight requirements.

You now know a few of the plants to grow, and you have some rudimentary knowledge of what it takes to grow plants.

WHERE TO GET PLANTS

Annuals and perennials (most of our cut flowers) are available as prestarted plants at nurseries at seasonal times. For convenience, many people buy these prestarted plants and simply put them in the ground and water them. The prestarts are available in six-packs or in boxes of twelve. Some come in a "flat": about twenty-five seedlings to a wooden, flat crate.

The advantage of prestarts is, as mentioned, convenience. You do not have to start seed and nurture plants along; they have passed the crucial stage of germination and are already growing. The disadvantage is that they are more costly than plants started from seed, and with pre-starts you are restricted to what is available. (No nursery could carry every variety of a certain plant group.)

Years ago I started all my plants from seed, but today I buy a great many prestarts. It is easier and saves time. But for those who have the time and want to grow their own plants from seed, by all means do it. There is a certain satisfaction in nurturing a tiny seed into a full-fledged plant that you do not get with started plants. And basically (if you have time), starting seed is really easy. We cover this phase of growing in detail in Chapter 7.

Seeds are purchased in packages at nurseries or can be ordered from mail-order suppliers.

Bulbs are also available already started, or you can start them yourself. In this case I prefer starting the plant from the bulb; it is easy and takes little time. With bulbs, the flowers are already formed in the bulb and need only water and sun to bring them to fruition. Bulbs are discussed in Chapter 6.

WHY GROW YOUR OWN?

If you have ever purchased flowers, you will know why it makes good sense to grow your own. The cost of most florists' blooms is high, and having flowers for arrangements or just as spot color in the home does much to create a pleasant ambience in the home. There is a psychological lift besides a financial gain.

The flowers you grow yourself will also last much longer than any flowers you purchase, for an obvious reason: those purchased are already several days old; thus, your own flowers, freshly cut, last and last—it is not uncommon to have roses and daisies last for ten days.

Cutting some colorful flowers can bring you out of the doldrums, and then the colorful arrangements in the house maintain that cheerful character lacking in so many rooms.

2

Where to Have the Flower Garden

GENERALLY, gardens that were popular years ago were ornamental and utilitarian. They included not only beautiful flowers but herbs and vegetables that provided good food. The sites were usually out of view of the casual visitor, tucked away in some remote, but convenient, areas of the property. Of course, those were the days when land was cheap, so many people could afford to have a fair amount of property. But today, with the cost of land and its concomitant taxes steadily rising, and at a very rapid rate, few of us can afford the luxury of several gardens, one here and one there, one for show, one for cutting. However, even in small areas, with some ingenuity you can design your cut flower garden to integrate into almost any situation. If you plant enough, there will be flowers for the garden and flowers for the house. And even though you may have to squeeze in room for flowers, the total look of the garden can be attractive rather than overgrown or almost barren. In fact, even on your rooftop you can have an appealing show of color, as you are about to discover.

BACKYARDS/SIDE YARDS

Most people's property includes a backyard, small though it may be, and here is a fine place for growing annuals and perennials. You can take a corner, say about 10 × 20 feet, and still have some flowers for the table. Do not, however, expect a year-round harvest from this or any small plot; those pictures in magazines of a spring-summer-fall garden are pretty, but such gardens require a great deal of work and money. Be content with some flowers in the spring and summer. If you want fall blooms, grow some suitable flowers in another separate, small garden in the backyard.

Locate the cutting garden where it will be accessible because a garden a far piece from the house is a bother. Make it easy for yourself to get to and from the garden; you will want to get to and from it so that you can care for it, cut flowers in it, and simply enjoy looking at it.

If your backyard already has ornamentals or a fine lawn, that is, if you already have a well-landscaped garden and now want to add a cutting garden, consider partitioning a sunny corner of the already established garden with some

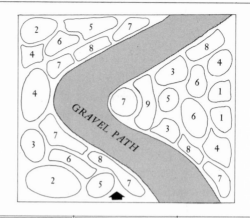

1. Rosa "Dainty Bess"   2. Rosa "Lilac Charm"   3. Rosa "Town Crier"

4. Geum   5. Chrys. "Pancho"   6. T. "Diamond Jubilee"

7. Zinnia "Mini-Pink"   8. Ageratum "Blue Mink"   9. Chrys. maximum

SIDEYARD GARDEN

CAROL CARLSON

tall shrubbery at one side. This will blend the flower garden into the landscape so it will look like an integral part of it, rather than a tacked-on afterthought. Or, if the main garden has a clump of small trees, plant some flowers and bulbs to the side of the trees (*not* under the trees, because flowers need sun).

If you are starting a whole new garden, I offer the same advice: Make the cutting garden part of the general landscape scheme. Again, this means the flower garden will be in a corner, perhaps bordered with some shrubs. Or, the cutting garden can be a wide strip at the very rear of the property. In this way it can still be part of the overall appearance of the land rather than a detraction from it. The main point, I think, is not to make the flower garden the focal point of any landscape plan.

On the other hand, you can locate the cutting garden close to the back door; in this position it will not diminish the rest of the garden. It will be, in itself, a separate entity close to the house, with the ornamental garden beyond. (And by being close to the back door, the flower garden is easier to tend and see.) Thus, the cutting garden should be in a not-too-distant corner, along the rear of the yard, or near the back door. These three spots are the ideal locations for your cutting garden.

FRONT YARDS

Most houses have either a front yard or a backyard. The cutting garden situated at the front of the house can be as handsome as one in the rear.

For an example, let us consider my own cutting garden, where I grow dozens of flowers and some herbs. The garden is across the driveway in a secluded spot that gets a lot of sun, and is on a slight slope that has good drainage. I merely walk across the driveway to enter my world of flowers. Yet my garden is an integrated part of my total landscape plan: my ornamental garden runs lengthwise in a semicircle, starting on the other side of the driveway.

I have a rather large front yard, about 180 feet across, so sectioning it is easy. But let us say that your front yard is small, 25 × 50 feet. In this case treat the flower garden as an entity; do *not*, as some gardeners might suggest, make it a part of any existing garden of trees and shrubs. If you do, the flowers' colors will become the accent of the ornamental garden, and then you will not want to pick the flowers. Again, make the garden an entity within an entity—separate and yet part of the garden.

PATIOS

The patio is another place where you can have a garden, and while this is not the ideal location, some plants for cutting can be grown in containers (see next chapter). Use large boxes and planters and select flowers that are sure to grow, such as petunias and zinnias. It is best to plant each box with a particular kind of flower rather than have several plants to a box—this way you get a concentration of color and also a nice decorative accent to enhance the patio area.

Position the containers at one end of the patio, in an L-shape perhaps, so they are out of the way of foot traffic and yet visible to the guest. A single row of containers along one length of the patio rarely looks good. Rather, stack and group boxes for a pleasing effect. The garden

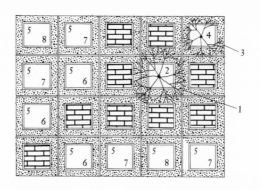

1. Rosa "Chrysler Imperial"		2. Aster "Blue Radiance"
3. Paeonia "Yachiyot Subaki"		4. Dianthus "Snowflake"
5. Echinacea "The King"		6. Ageratum "Summer Snow"
7. Dahlia "Vicki Ann"		8. Dahlia "Color Sketch"

ROOFTOP OR PATIO GARDEN

CAROL CARLSON

of boxes may be set on the ground outside the patio surface (usually paved) or directly on the paved surface. Work out the arrangements of the planter layout before you put soil and plants in the containers. This method eliminates moving heavy boxes.

If it is a new patio, by all means allow ground space (called planting pockets) within the paved area. This creates a handsome effect and appears more natural than a garden in boxes.

ROOFTOPS

Rooftop gardens are becoming more and more popular because this is space that generally goes unused. And gardens on rooftops contribute much to everyone's view; attractive plants replace dreary scenes of clotheslines, TV antennas, and debris. A rooftop garden can be a physical retreat for you and a visual treat for the neighbors. And here we are referring to any rooftop with a flat expanse such as on a garage roof, or on an apartment house roof. We are not thinking of that luxurious and expensive penthouse roof garden. Rooftops, no matter what they cover, are for everyone.

The cutting garden works well on a rooftop because a rooftop usually has more space than a patio. And by its very nature a rooftop generally is already sectioned; it usually has four sides, thus providing a separate place where you can put in a cutting garden by using one side of the total footage. However, as with a patio, on a rooftop the flower garden must be grown in boxes and planters. You cannot just dump a load of soil on a roof and start gardening (for one thing, the weight of the soil would probably cause the roof to collapse, especially when you add water to the soil). Rooftop gardens have to be container gardens.

NO MATTER
WHERE YOU PUT IT

I will say the following here and repeat it several times throughout the book because it is so important: cutting gardens need a sunny spot, at least four hours of sun daily; and six hours are better. Forget trying to grow flowers in shady places because there they will not bloom profusely. Although the idea of that shady garden is romantic, it is not practical for flowers. Accept what you can do rather than hit your head against a garden wall. Annuals and perennials, which constitute most of the cutting flowers we discuss, do require sun, and lots of it. But luckily, every garden location, whether on a rooftop or in a backyard or front yard, has one sunny place—this is the spot for the cutting garden, not any other area.

GARDEN PLANNING

We have talked about where to put your cutting garden—backyard, rooftop, patio, for example. Now let's look at how to plan a cutting garden. As previously mentioned, you will want your space for flowers in an area by itself. And this entity of color can be small or large depending on how much space you have for it.

If you will look at our three garden-plan drawings you will see specific arrangements of flowers along with suggested places for the garden. If your area is small, reduce the quantity of flowers in each group; if it is large, increase the number of flowers in each group.

PREPARATION/LOCATION

If you are using an existing area of the garden, spade and till the soil—break it up and add fresh topsoil to it. Just how much topsoil you add to the garden site depends upon specific space, but generally a 2- to 3-inch layer of new soil worked into existing soil will make the planting area a good place to grow plants. See Chapter 4 for more information on soils.

The cutting garden will need good drainage; annuals and perennials grow fast and need lots of water; so, again, prepare the site carefully. Be sure the soil is porous and excess water drains away.

If possible, select a place for your garden that has sun. Beware of small trees that will rob the area of light. A few small trees are fine but large shade trees block out light and the flower harvest will be sparse. Wind can be a problem in some gardens, too, so plan for windbreaks. Place shrubs as hedges and barriers at the point where storms strike your property.

PATHS AND WALKS

A garden you can't walk into is more of a nuisance than a joy, so no matter where you have the garden, be sure you can get into it. That means you should have suitable paths and walks. This will make it easy to tend the flowers and to cut them.

Paths may be cleared areas covered with gravel or fir bark or they may be of earth. My cutting garden has brick paths simply because I had an excess number of bricks on hand. The idea is to be able to get to your flowers—easily.

3

A
Movable
Feast

FOR YOUR FLOWER GARDENS on the rooftop or patio you are going to have to grow the plants in various kinds of containers: tubes, boxes, planters, and pots. As you know from growing houseplants in containers, the care of container plants is a bit different than for plants growing in the ground. You also have to have the right-sized containers for plants, and the containers, since they will be on view, have to look nice. Here we shall tell you all about containers—how to build them or what kind of commercially made ones to use—and how to properly care for your confined flowering plants. We shall also cover the arrangement of containers—how to place them so that they will add to, rather than detract from, your cutting garden.

BUILDING CONTAINERS

If you have a garage, basement, toolshed, or any area where you can do some carpentry, you can build your own useful and attractive wood containers. Believe me, this is not hard to do, and the results will please both you and your plants.

To start, buy some redwood or cedar. Each type of wood ages beautifully and, more importantly, resists the harsh effects of rain, wind, and sun. Woods less expensive are pine or Douglas fir. These woods are satisfactory *only* if you paint them or put on a preservative. Otherwise, the rain and sun will mildew, warp, and rot the wood (and invite insects). An oil-base enamel (rather than a latex, or water-base, enamel) is ideal paint to use and can be of any color; check at your hardware store for preservatives (ask a knowledgeable clerk for advice if you are confused).

The cheapest way to buy wood is in stock sizes and then cut it to your containers' dimensions at home. But if you do not have the time or the inclination and are willing to spend some extra money, have the lumber dealer cut the wood to your specifications.

If you buy stock sizes, you have to keep in mind several important things. First, stock sizes are *not* true sizes. In other words, a 2×4-inch board is really only $1\frac{1}{2} \times 3\frac{1}{2}$ inches, or slightly smaller, say $1\frac{3}{8} \times 3\frac{3}{8}$. You have to consider the true board-sizes when planning your carpentry, or your containers will never materialize because nothing will fit! Second, pieces of wood smaller than 2×4 inches are referred to by lumber dealers as strips: 2 × 3s, or 1 × 2s, and so on. Third, posts (which you may need for container construction) are either 2 or 4 inches square. Finally, when you buy wood, always give the dealer the dimensions in the following order: thickness, width, and length; then indicate what type of wood you want, such as redwood; and lastly, the grade, such as construction grade, kiln-dried, or rough. (Construction grade is fine and less expensive than other grades for containers.)

The detailing has to depend upon the container's size; proportion and symmetry should also be considered. For example, detail large containers with big pieces of wood; detail small containers with finer, smaller pieces or strips of wood.

You can build planters or square cubes. Planters are long and narrow, like a windowbox, but larger. Plan the design of the planter carefully so it will coordinate with the plants. In other words, small planters look best with small plants, large ones with big plants. A good, average size for a planter is 12 inches wide, 10 inches deep, and 36 inches long. Build larger or smaller planters depending upon the size of the flowering plants you will be growing. Use 2 × 4-, 1 × 12-, or 2 × 12-inch lumber. Note that you should elevate planters with 2-inch blocks under each corner so that air can enter the box from underneath. This will eliminate hiding places for insects.

Square cubes are dramatic as containers. They can be stacked, aligned horizontally, or placed randomly. A practical size is 20 × 20 inches. Use 2 × 4-, 1 × 12-, or 2 × 12-inch lumber, as for the rectangular planter.

Now that you have built your containers, give them a finished, custom-made look by adding some final touches of detailing. For example, add wood strips, score the container, or sandblast. With wood strips nailed or glued to the outside of the container you can form lattice- and diamond-type designs. Or, outline the container with a raised rectangle. This creates a shadowbox effect. (The average-sized container will need 16 pieces of 1 × 2-inch strips of wood.) Or, simply place wood strips ½ inch apart, vertically or horizontally, on the outside of a simple cube. This covers any mistakes and creates a finished look.

You can score a container with a wood chisel. For example, for a bas-relief look, score ¼-inch deep lines, and space the lines ½ to 1 inch apart, vertically or horizontally, on the outside of the container.

Sandblasting adds a textured, handsome look to a container; rent a sanding machine. You can also sand the wood by hand to a lustrous, smooth finish.

If you detail your wood containers, always add a molding, or cap, to the top. This finishes the container and adds dimension. Caps are usually 1 × 3 inches; nail them in place, letting the outer edge overhang the container by ½ to 1 inch.

COMMERCIAL CONTAINERS

If you live in an apartment, it is difficult to build containers —there simply is not space, or, many times, you just might not have time to do a custom planter. You can still, however, have your flowers on rooftops or terraces by buying containers. Nurseries have many types of wooden planters —none, I'm afraid, inexpensive, but they do last for many years. The standard planter is about 10 inches wide by 36 inches long and can accommodate many plants—you can certainly grow petunias, some cosmos, and baby's breath, for example, in these containers.

In addition to the long, narrow, wooden planter, wooden boxes ranging in size from 10 inches square to 28 inches square are also available. These too can be used for cut flowers, and placed properly, even in a small space, they can create a handsome garden.

Wine barrels (sawn in half), and soy kegs, and various other housings for plants are also sold, and of course the standard clay pot can also be used successfully to grow your flowers. These now come in a wide range of sizes from 5 inches to 28 inches in diameter. The big clay pots are heavy, so be prepared to handle their weight by having a friend around to help you.

Household containers like crocks and cans are often suggested by various people for plants, but actually, these are better used indoors for houseplants. Outdoors, they do not look that good, and most are simply not large enough to accommodate many plants. You want to grow at least four or five different plants for your cut flowers.

For growing cut-flower plants, first consider the wooden planter and box, then the clay pots.

Plastic planters are used too, but these usually require careful watering, and to my eye do not have the appeal of wooden containers. Plastic holds water longer than clay or wood, and this can be a disadvantage because too much waste can sour soil and harm plants.

CARE OF
CONTAINER PLANTS

As we said in the beginning of this chapter, container plants, like houseplants, have to be cared for slightly differently than plants in the ground. The slight differences are feeding and watering. In a container, plants have smaller

GRAVEL PATHWAY

1. Lathyrus "Spencer's Giant"

2. Dianthus barbatus

3. Rudbeckia gloriosa

4. Dahlia (pompom type)

5. Tropaeolum "Glorious Gleam"

6. Tagetes "Cream Puff"

7. Salpiglossis "Splash"

8. Chrys. Thomas Killin

CONTAINER GARDEN

CAROL CARLSON

amounts of soil, and so the soil dries out faster than soil in the ground. Also, because soil is confined within a container, water stays in the soil, in the small area of the planter, if the container has no drainage holes. Thus, you have to water your container plants more often than plants in the ground, and you *must* have drainage holes in the container.

Now that you know that you have to water your plants in containers more often, you are probably wondering when to water. And you should be considering the results of overwatering: the soil turns sour and harms plants. Before blindly planting your container, put a 1- to 2-inch layer of gravel over the drainage holes, add 5 or 6 inches of rich soil, and then add a handful or two of charcoal chips. The gravel will help prevent the soil from turning sour if you overwater: excess water will spread out through the gravel and thus have more space to evaporate. The charcoal chips further ensure that the soil will not turn sour from excess watering because charcoal will neutralize the acidity of the overwatered soil.

Water plants in containers three times a week during the growing months, twice a week otherwise. Naturally, you can decrease this watering schedule if your area gets sufficient rainfall and the boxes are where rain can strike them. No matter what, just be sure the soil is always evenly moist because annuals and perennials thrive on lots of water.

Feeding plants in containers is different than feeding plants in the ground because, in the ground, excess salts can leach into the soil, but in containers they are confined to the planter. And too much toxic salt can harm plants. Thus, you have to feed container plants very carefully. Use a 10–10–5 plant food every other watering during the growing season; never feed young plants too much—let them grow two weeks before the first application of plant food. And do not feed plants in soil that is dry; the soil should be moderately moist. (More about plant foods in the following chapter.)

4

Primer
of Flower
Culture

ANY GARDEN needs the right soil, air, light, water, food, and insect and disease protection if it is to perform to its fullest ability. And you need the right combination of these factors if your flower garden is to bloom profusely. Thus, you may not hit the combination until the second year rather than the first; so if bloom is not what you expect the first year, don't give up. This chapter, plus some persistence on your part, should result in good growing.

AIR

Soil has to have sufficient air circulating through it because the air ensures the passage of essential gases through the soil. Air also influences the rate of water loss from a plant—the drier the air, the more water is lost. If water loss is too great, the plants may wither and die. Too much air, in the form of wind, increases the rate of water loss, thus modifying the water content of plants' cells and affecting their growth.

LIGHT

Outdoor flowers must have four to six hours of light each day because light affects the photosynthesis and chlorophyll-production processes.

WATER

Flowering plants must have enough water or they will not do well. (And if these plants are healthy, they can consume a great deal of water.) Water, as a solvent, holds nutrients so that plants can then draw the nourishment into their systems. Water also carries off plant waste-products as it evaporates from leaf surfaces, and is essential for photosynthesis.

SOIL

The test of good soil is its porosity and tilth (physical structure), as well as its nutrient content. Good soil must have air spaces. Hard soil is poor; water cannot pass through it and so accumulates on top of it. If the soil is too soft (sandy), it cannot hold moisture long enough for plants to use it—the water runs right through it and out.

Clay soil is heavy; it is hard to work with; it warms up slowly in the spring, when plants are eager to grow; it forms a crust, so air and water cannot reach the roots of plants; and it has to be tilled. Because sandy soil does not hold moisture, many of the soluble plant foods essential to plants' growth are immediately lost. Clay or sandy soil must be improved; you must add nutrients to it. (*Note:* Never use what are called soil conditioners. True, they will improve the soil's tilth, but not the soil's nutrition.)

SOIL NUTRIENTS

Humus is animal manure, leaf mold, or any decayed *organic* (living) matter. Whether you use inorganic or organic plant foods, perennials and annuals need feeding when they start growth in spring and through the summer while they are actively growing. (A 10–10–5 food is good for flowers.) Here are more hints to help you feed plants: (1) use a weak solution rather than a massive dose; (2) never feed a sick plant; (3) decrease (gradually) feeding when cold weather starts; (4) increase feeding as weather warms up; (5) never feed newly planted prestarts or transplants.

Humus adds nutrients to the soil, nourishes microorganisms and lightens clay soil so that it holds moisture or improves the tilth of sandy soil. Humus is constantly being used and depleted, so it must be replaced at least once a year. You will have to be your own judge as to how much humus to add to soil. I use about 1 inch of humus to 6 inches of soil, which has proved satisfactory for my garden.

Compost is decayed vegetable matter like kitchen garbage, grass clippings, leaves, and twigs. It is a good idea to start a compost pile on your property if you have the space. Make a bin from 4 × 4 inch posts and 2 × 12 inch boards. Place one board on top of the other and attach horizontally to the posts to contain the compost pile; leave a gate on the bin. (Suppliers sell commercially made metal bins.)

Start the compost pile by throwing in twigs, leaves, grass clippings, garden debris, and kitchen garbage. When the pile has some depth, add some manure and a sprinkling of lime. Keep the pile moist, but never saturated. After a few months, turn the heap, bringing the sides to the top.

PLANT FOODS

Plants must have fair amounts of nitrogen, phosphorus, and potassium; smaller amounts of iron, boron, manganese, zinc, and other trace elements. Nitrogen stimulates plants' development and is necessary for the healthy growth of stems and leaves. Phosphorus promotes good root development. And potassium adds to the general vigor of a plant while acting as a balancing influence on other plant nutrients.

You can buy plant foods at nurseries, supermarkets, and so on. The ingredients are numerically listed on the package, bottle, or can: the first numeral denotes the percentage of nitrogen; the second, the amount of phosphorus; and the third, the potassium content. These commercially packaged, synthetic (chemical, thus inorganic) fertilizers are available in four forms: powder, pellets, tablets, liquid. Powdered foods or fertilizers can simply be sprinkled on the soil; then add water. Pellets are spread around the plant, and then the soil is watered. Concentrated tablets have to be dissolved in water before they can be poured on the soil. Concentrated liquids are also mixed with water, but they have to be sprayed on the soil with special spraying equipment.

Instead of the inorganic fertilizers, you can use organic fertilizers, which contain nitrogen that is slowly released over relatively long periods. Nitrogen-containing materials depend upon soil bacteria to decompose and transform the resultant compounds into a nitrogen form available to the plant. Organic foods are manure, cottonseed meal, and animal and vegetable tankage.

MULCHING

Mulch is a rather inappropriate word in the gardener's lexicon. It sounds like eating. Actually, a mulch is really a protective coating (insulator) to protect plants from alternately freezing and thawing. It helps keep soil warm during the cold spells so that plant roots do not freeze. Mulch also helps to prevent weeds and retains moisture for plants. Many people swear by mulching, and it is a good practice, one which you can certainly use for your perennials and bulbs to protect them from winter's grip.

Apply mulch after the ground has frozen; some gardeners leave it on all year; others remove it come spring. I am one of the latter kind of gardeners because I do not want my plants kept too moist (this sometimes can lead to crown rot). There are various kinds of mulch, anything from newspapers to aluminum foil, but I prefer the organic mulches; these eventually decay and add nutrients to the soil. Good organic mulches for plants are leaves, hay and straw, grass clippings, ground fir-bark, sawdust, and pecan or peanut shells.

I generally use ground fir-bark because it is a convenient type of mulch that looks attractive. It is available in bags and, at this writing, is not exorbitantly priced. Apply any mulch in a layer 2 to 4 inches thick around the collar of the plant.

PLANT PESTS

Observation is one of the main keys to controlling harmful garden insects. Even the novice strolling around his property can prevent trouble from starting if he knows what to look for. Plants often develop symptoms which indicate that all is not well with them. Even though some of these symptoms are easily recognized, others may be inconspicuous. Yet constant observation is the best protection against plant pests.

When a plant is not doing well, but culture is reasonably good, you should look for insects. Sometimes the culprits can be seen with a magnifying glass, but at other times they may be invisible and can only be diagnosed by a specialist. So before you decide what to do about an insect pest, you must identify it. If you can recognize the tiny, black, oval eggs of aphids, you can do something about them before the attack becomes a massacre.

Many insects lay eggs that will provide food for their hatching young, but some (and aphids are a good example) produce living young. In their immature stages, insects grow by a process called molting—the periodic shedding of their outer skin. The insects change gradually as each molting occurs, and in this stage and until they mature, are called nymphs.

Nymphs have coloring different from the adults, but they

retain the same habits and appendages. Nymphs may be wingless or winged when mature, depending on their species. Sometimes the insect may be represented by both winged and wingless adults. However, once the wings have developed, the insect stops growing and is considered mature. All plant-sucking insects and some chewing ones go through this gradual transformation. Of course, if we can destroy the eggs of these insects before they mature (that is, in their egg or nymph stages), so much the better.

Some insects upon maturation hardly look as they did when young. There is a complete transformation, and the eggs hatch into a wormlike stage called larva. (In many groups, even the plants they feed on differ in the larval and adult stages.) Mature beetles are known as grubs in the larval stage. Caterpillar is the young stage for moths, butterflies, and sawflies; wireworms are the larvae of click beetles.

Larvae are heavy feeders, and, as mentioned, they grow by molting. When they reach their full size, they go into an inactive, nonfeeding period called a pupa; in this stage they are often protected by a cocoon or chrysalis. (You have probably seen pupae in the woods or in your garden.) This is the time when they undergo an amazing transformation, finally emerging as full-fledged adults.

You can find larvae on the trees or plants on which they feed, although oftentimes they go into the soil. All larvae have a chewing-type mouth that makes it easy for them to eat quickly and voraciously.

INSECT-CHEWERS

Chewing insects are fast feeders equipped with powerful jaws that allow them to rip and tear edges of leaves, make holes, or skeletonize foliage. These insects range from many forms of caterpillars to the numerous kinds of beetles and their grublike larvae. Cabbage worms eat large holes in leaves. The elm leaf beetle and Japanese beetle skeletonize the leaf, and many caterpillars, sawflies, and other insects feed at the edge of the leaf. Some larvae have a protective coloration that makes it difficult to see them.

SAP-FEEDERS

Sap-sucking insects are devastating because they can attack a plant from the stem to the growing tips to the roots. They have a needlelike appendage called the proboscis that they insert into the plant part and use to suck out juices. Just the insertion of the proboscis can weaken a plant severely enough to make it prone to attack by other pests that feed on sickly plants. Furthermore, some sap-sucking insects often transmit viruses to the plants they attack.

Like the chewing insects whose damage is seen in scalloped leaves and holes in foliage, the sap-sucking insects can be recognized by the harm they do. Leaves become yellow or stippled, brown or wilted. Dieback of twigs and branches is often seen, and frequently, sticky honeydew and sooty mold cover the leaves and branches. The most common sap-sucking insects are aphids, leafhoppers, lace bugs, scale insects, mealybugs, whiteflies, thrips, and plant bugs.

APHIDS

Aphids are sometimes called plant lice, and they can wreak havoc in a garden. They do their damage by piercing stems, leaves, buds, practically all parts of a plant, with elongated mouthparts called stylets; then they extract vital plant juices. The result is that leaves curl and growth is stunted or stopped. Where there is a heavy aphid infestation, the plant usually dies. In addition, aphids also can introduce virus diseases into the garden, and these diseases can, in some cases, be more damaging to plants than the aphids.

Aphids breed incredibly fast and in large numbers, and in warm climates they reproduce continuously. Some aphids do not have wings, but others do, and they migrate to other plants, starting new colonies. There are many different kinds of aphids, but generally most are black or green, occasionally red. There are pea aphids, melon aphids, plant aphids, bean aphids, and so forth.

The aphid is really a triple threat in the garden: it is destructive in itself; it introduces bacterial diseases; and it gives off from the tip of its abdomen a sweet secretion that is a favorite food of some ants. These ants move the aphids about to productive plants and protect them in their own nests at night or when the weather is bad. Generally, where there are ants, there will soon be aphids, so take precautionary steps to eliminate ants as soon as you see them. (Ladybugs and praying mantids are excellent aphid predators.) You can use a soapy solution of half water and half detergent to thwart the pests.

THRIPS

Thrips are slender, needlelike, winged insects that scrape stems or leaves of a plant and then suck out plant sap. Their nymphs are wingless. Thrips hibernate in winter, but when warm weather comes they start feeding on young plants. They can produce a new generation every two weeks in hot weather, so do not let them get established. Use insect predators (available from suppliers) for control, or spray plants with a blast of water.

SCALE

Scale, an insect commonly found on shrubs and flowers, is less known than aphids or mealybugs, and yet it does considerable damage in the garden. Scale are either soft-shelled or, in most cases, have an armored, covered hull, and they are difficult to eliminate because they stick stubbornly to leaves and stems. They suck sap from the plant and can kill a healthy specimen in short order unless they are checked. Further, like the other notorious garden pests, aphids and thrips, they produce honeydew that attracts ants. Scrape off scale with toothpicks or use cotton swabs soaked in alcohol.

MEALYBUGS

Mealybugs are white, cottony, tiny insects that hide in the leaf axils of a plant. They form colonies and can rapidly ruin a plant if they are not eliminated quickly. The male of the species can fly; females are wingless. For mild infestations, use cotton swabs dipped in alcohol; in other cases, use natural preventatives.

NATURAL PREVENTATIVES

Predatory insects and birds will, to a great extent, help to keep the garden generally insect-free. But there are other natural defenses that are simple and easy that we can use too. These include companion planting, botanical repellents, and some good old-fashioned remedies that many of us remember.

Any garden with a concentration of one particular plant is an invitation to insects. However, if you mix your plantings, or companion plant, as it is called, there will be less

chance of pests invading your garden. Nasturtiums repel
aphids, and it's a simple matter to scatter some seeds.
Tansy, a pretty herb, discourages cutworms and cabbage
worms. Rue, a hardy evergreen plant, is so noxious to insects
that they will not touch it or any plants growing near it.
Marigolds and asters deter insects too, to some degree. But
the most popular plants that repel are garlic and chives.
Certainly these are easily grown and are not objectionable
in the flower garden.

What is the repellent quality of these companion plants?
With most of them the leaves have a disagreeable odor or a
bitter taste. With some, it is the color that deters the insects.
A prime example of this is the orange nasturtium.

As mentioned, chemical sprays should be avoided in
the garden. However, botanical insecticides—pyrethrum,
rotenone, quassia, and ryania—are not persistent and are
not harmful to man or earth. They are botanical repellents
made from various plants and are now available as packaged
insecticides.

Pyrethrum kills, on contact, aphids, whiteflies, leafhoppers, and thrips. Rotenone wards off spider mite, chinch
bug, aphids, and the common housefly. Ryania, although
not lethal, incapacitates (perhaps by paralysis) Japanese
beetle, elm leaf beetle, and cabbage looper. More and more
of the chemical companies that formerly used deadly
poisons for garden protection are now marketing these
natural repellents. However, check contents on packages
carefully to be sure persistent poisons are not added.

Before leaving botanical repellents let us look at a very
old one—nicotine—which is available as nicotine sulfate. This
is a poisonous alkaloid for insects, and it is highly toxic
to mammals. However, it dissipates rapidly and is effective

against aphids, whitefly, leafhopper, and dozens of other pests. If your garden is attacked by a heavy infestation of insects (and this would be rare), occasionally use the nicotine solution if you deem it necessary.

If you can bring yourself to touch insects, handpicking is still an effective way of ridding the small garden of pests. This of course will work for large insects, but for pests such as aphids and spider mites you will have to resort to the old-fashioned solution of laundry soap and water. Use a half-pound of laundry soap to two gallons of water, spray plants, and then hose them with clear water. This preparation will also eliminate red spider, mealybug, and scale. Don't expect a miracle though, since it takes several sprayings to really beat the insects; but rather than having to use poisons, it is well worth the trouble.

INSECTICIDE CHART

INSECTS	WHAT THEY LOOK LIKE	WHAT THEY ATTACK	WHAT THEY DO	CHEMICAL CONTROL
Aphids	Green, black, pink, yellow, or red soft-bodied insects	Almost all plants	Stunt plants and deform leaves	Malathion, rotenone
Lace bugs	Small bugs with large, lacy wings	Azaleas, oaks, birches, hawthorn, and other plants	Make leaves appear mottled	Malathion

INSECTS	WHAT THEY LOOK LIKE	WHAT THEY ATTACK	WHAT THEY DO	CHEMICAL CONTROL
Leafhoppers	Wedge-shaped insects that hop	Many plants	Make leaves pale or brown, and stunt plants	Pyrethrum, Malathion
Mealybugs	White, cottony insects	Many plants	Stunt plants, so they don't grow	Sevin, Diazinon
Mites	Minute sucking insects	Almost all plants	Discolor leaves	Diazinon
Nematodes	Microscopic worms	Many plants	Stunt plants and cause them to die back	Sterilize soil
Scale	Tiny, usually hard, oval insects	Many plants	Cause yellowing or loss of leaves	Diazinon
Snails, slugs (not insects, but common pests)	Easily recognized	Many plants	Eat foliage	Any snail bait without metaldehyde (Snare-All is fine)
Thrips	Tiny, winged insects	Few plants	Cause leaves to become silvery	Malathion
Wireworm	Hard and shiny coiled worms	Flowers and vegetables	Kill seedlings; work underground	Diazinon

NOTES ON INSECTICIDES

Malathion—safest for humans and pets

Sevin—a carbonate, one of the safest of synthetics

Diazinon—very toxic

Systemics—highly toxic (cumulative and persistent effects not yet proven)

Metaldehyde—Do not use. It contains arsenic.

Check with your local agricultural station (listed by county in your telephone book) for further information on insects in your area and suggestions for eliminating them.

5

Annuals
and
Perennials

ANNUALS, which bloom once and then die, are the mainstay of the garden, whether you use them for outdoor display or grow them for indoor cut-flower beauty. And raising annuals costs little; a twenty-five-cent packet will supply you with hundreds of plants. Most annuals have a long season of bloom, and, of course, as cut flowers they are indispensable. Marigolds and calendulas, China asters, sweet peas, to name a few, can bring handsome color to the indoors from summer to late fall, almost for pennies.

Some people like to have annuals in the garden plan just

for color; they never cut them. If you have enough space you will probably do this, adding to the cutting garden in some other area—a few rows in the vegetable garden or maybe lining a walk.

Perennials *are the backbone* of the garden. They bloom, die down, and then start growing again the following year. Some perennials, like peonies, live for many years, but others, like delphiniums, live only two or three years. They are thus timesavers, but remember that perennials are not at their best until their second or third season; so for ready color, grow annuals.

Between annuals and perennials are the group of plants called biennials, which last for two years. They make roots and leaves the first season and bear flowers the second season.

GROWING ANNUALS AND PERENNIALS

Annuals and perennials need as much sun as they can get and a reasonably light, deeply drained, neutral, porous soil. If you furnish sun and soil, the rest is easy, provided you follow good culture habits.

Water annuals and perennials whenever the surface looks dry, every day or every other day in warm weather depending upon rainfall. And water deeply (slowly, but for a long time); it takes three hours to soak eight inches of soil. Keep weeds out of the flower beds by removing them by hand or by mulching (smothering) the area thoroughly. *Never* use weed killers.

Make sure the soil area or the soil in containers is well prepared for your annuals and perennials (see Chapter 7, Step 3, for preparing the soil for seedlings). Label your plants so you know what you have, and stake tall growers (wind can destroy plants). Always watch for insects and signs of disease or culture problems; and feed flowers only after they have started growth. Finally, remove dead flowers.

LIST OF ANNUALS

Annuals and perennials marked with an asterisk (*) in the following lists are described later in more detail.

AGERATUM, FLOSSFLOWER (*Ageratum houstonianum*). These are available in blue, white, or pink varieties, blooming from early summer until fall. The plant ranges from 2 to 22 inches in height.

ALYSSUM (*Lobularia maritima*). Available in several colors, this low-growing annual is an ideal edging plant. It also has a multitude of other uses in the garden when it is combined with other plants or used as filler around perennials.

*ASTER; China Aster (*Callistephus chinenesis*). This is one of the best flowers for the cutting garden; floriferous, easy to grow, and pretty.

*BACHELOR'S BUTTON, CORNFLOWER (*Centaurea cyanus*). These fine plants bear pink, white, wine, or blue flowers.

*CALENDULA, POT MARIGOLD (*Calendula officinalis*). This plant is hard to beat; it grows with almost no care.

CANDYTUFT (*Iberis umbellata*). Masses of flowers in pink, salmon, or white make candytuft a good choice for the beginning gardener. Plants mount to 12 or 15 inches, and in late spring and early summer they bloom their heads off. This is a good plant for both cutting or display gardens.

COSMOS. These grow easily in almost any situation. Lovely flowers of red, pink, white, yellow. Beautiful in summer; fine for cutting.

DIANTHUS (pinks). Because they bloom over a long period, these are valuable in the cutting garden. They come in a wide range of colors and varieties, with the deep crimson tones perhaps the most popular.

IMPATIENS (*Impatiens balsamina*). Get to know these plants because they have many virtues in the garden; they come in many different colors and heights and bloom profusely. They can succeed in shade.

MARIGOLD (*Tagetes erecta*). These all-time favorites are the backbone of a garden. Plants grow quickly, come in all sizes from 6 to 40 inches, and constantly bloom in many shades of yellow, orange, dark red, and maroon from summer to fall. The plants can be grown by themselves for lovely accents or with other plantings. There are many types of marigolds: French dwarf, which grows to 18 inches and comes in many colors; and African dwarf, which grows to 16 inches.

NASTURTIUM (*Tropaeolum majus*). The underrated nasturtiums can bring vivid yellow, orange, crimson, pink, maroon, and multicolors to the garden, and easier plants to grow cannot be found. Nasturtiums bloom from early summer until frost, and now come in single, semidouble, or double flowers. The dwarf plants are good for borders, and the taller varieties provide nice spots of color. Most nasturtiums will crowd out weeds and grow rapidly with little care.

MOLUCELLA LAEVIS (Bells of Ireland) *top*

DIMORPHOTECA SINUATA (African daisy) *center*

PHLOX DRUMMONDII (Phlox, annual) *bottom*

DELPHINIUM AJACIS (Larkspur)   *top*

GAILLARDIA PULCHELLA   *center*

GOMPHRENA GLOBOSA (Globe amaranth)   *bottom*

LATHYRUS ODORATUS (Sweet pea)   *top*

NICOTIANA ALATA (Flowering tobacco)   *center*

NIGELLA DAMASCENA (Love in a mist)   *bottom*

Lᴜᴘɪɴᴜѕ Hᴀʀᴛᴡᴇɢɪɪ (Lupine, annual) *top*

Tʀᴏᴘᴀᴇᴏʟᴜᴍ Mᴀᴊᴜѕ (Nasturtium) *center*

Cᴀʟʟɪѕᴛᴇᴘʜᴜѕ Cʜɪɴᴇɴѕɪѕ (China aster) *bottom*

TAGETES ERECTA (African marigold)   *top*

TAGETES PATULA (French marigold)   *center*

TAGETES TENUIFOLIA SIGNATA (Signet marigold)   *bottom*

Tɪᴛʜᴏɴɪᴀ Rᴏᴛᴜɴᴅɪғᴏʟɪᴀ (Mexican sunflower) *top*

Lɪᴍᴏɴɪᴜᴍ Sɪɴᴜᴀᴛᴜᴍ (Statice) *center*

Vɪᴏʟᴀ Tʀɪᴄᴏʟᴏʀ Hᴏʀᴛᴇɴsɪs *bottom*

Cᴏsᴍᴏs Bɪᴘɪɴɴᴀᴛᴜs (Cosmos)   *top*

Cᴇɴᴛᴀᴜʀᴇᴀ Cʏᴀɴᴜs (Bachelor's button)   *center*

Cʟᴀʀᴋɪᴀ Aᴍᴏᴇɴᴀ (Farewell-to-Spring)   *bottom*

ANTIRRHINUM MAJUS (Snapdragon)   *top*

ARCTOTIS STOECHADIFOLIA GRANDIS (African daisy)   *center*

BROWALLIA AMERICANA   *bottom*

MATTHIOLA INCANA (Stock)   *top*

HELICHRYSUM BRACTEATUM (Strawflower)   *center*

NEMESIA STRUMOSA   *bottom*

Calendula Officinalis (Pot marigold)   *top*

Coreopsis Tinctoria   *center*

Gypsophila Elegans (Baby's breath)   *bottom*

PETUNIA. It is tough to beat these in the garden and they do make fine cut flowers. There are dozens of colors and varieties, and plants bloom easily in the sun with plenty of water. Prolific in summer. Use Grandiflora types for best flowering.

PHLOX (*Phlox drummondii*). These grow to 16 inches and have lovely clusters of 1-inch rose, crimson, salmon, white, scarlet, or violet flowers, often with contrasting eyes. The bloom is abundant, and plants are seldom bothered by insects. Phlox need sun and more sun.

*SNAPDRAGON (*Antirrhinum majus*). Tall, stately, and lovely, with beguiling flowers; there are many colors to choose from, except blue.

STOCK (Mathiola). Desirable flowers for cutting in many colors: white, pink, crimson, blue. Bloom over long period in summer. Giant Imperial stock exceptionally good.

*ZINNIA (*Zinnia elegans*). This popular flower has great diversity: many sizes, forms, heights, and colors (orange, yellow, pink, red, lavender, and some bicolors).

Here are some of the lesser-grown annuals that you can also use in your cutting garden: *Arctotis stoechadifolia grandis* is a formidable name for a very pretty yellow or pink flower. Sometimes called African daisy, Arctotis needs good sun and blooms in early spring. For something a little different you might want to try *Browallia americana*; this one has blue flowers—always welcome in a bouquet. *Molucella laevis*, known as bells-of-Ireland, offers green bell-like flowers and makes a dramatic statement in an arrangement. Flowering tobacco (Nicotiana) is another fine addition to the cutting garden.

Rarely seen in the cutting garden but certainly deserving of more attention are *Nemesia strumosa* and *Nigella damascena*. *Nemesia strumosa* is available in many flower-colors and is always pretty. The very fine *Nigella damascena*, known as love-in-a-mist, has airy blue, white, or rose flowers. Finally, don't pass up *Tithonia rotundifolia*, the Mexican sunflower, with its bright orange flowers.

LIST OF PERENNIALS

ASTER; NEW ENGLAND ASTER (*Aster frikartii*) (*Aster novae-angliae*). Their dramatic blue and purple flowers make these two fine perennials outstanding. The daisylike flowers, which are produced in abundance, are bright and showy. Plants are available in several heights and make fine displays.

BABY'S BREATH (*Gypsophila paniculata*). These dainty and lacy plants grow rapidly to 2 feet and bear lots of small, rounded white or pink-and-white flowers that last over a month.

BASKET OF GOLD (*Alyssum saxatile*). The golden flowers and gray foliage are a treat indoors and out. But do not confuse this plant with the annual sweet alyssum, which is technically named Lobularia.

BELLFLOWER (*Campanula persicifolia*). Bellflowers have white or blue flowers in June and July and grow to 10 inches. Give plants full sun or light shade, and be sure they are in well-drained soil.

BLANKETFLOWER (*Gaillardia aristata*). Gaillardias produce showy, daisylike, bright yellow or bronzy scarlet flowers over a long period of time. Undemanding, blanketflowers do best in a slightly sandy soil with adequate sun.

BUGLOSS (*Anchusa azurea*). Clusters of bright blue blossoms make bugloss an outstanding addition in the garden. The plants can grow to 6 feet , and some excellent new varieties are available.

*CHRYSANTHEMUM; SHASTA DAISY (*Chrysanthemum maximum; Chrysanthemum morifolium*). These are available in a multitude of shapes and colors: white to yellow, gold, or orange.

*DELPHINIUM; LARKSPUR (*Delphinium elatum*). Handsome, tall plants with white, pink, or blue flowers.

FALSE SPIREA (*Astilbe japonica*). For shady places; this plant has white, pink, or red flowers in the summer.

GLORIOSA DAISY (Rudbeckia). Easy-to-grow plants that bloom even in a shady place. Flowers generally yellow or gold. Grow to 30 inches. Very handsome and very good cut flowers. Summer-to-fall bloom.

JAPANESE ANEMONE (*Anemone japonica*). These are dramatic flowers—vivid red or blue—that bloom in fall. They grow 20 inches tall and are very attractive as a cut blossom.

MONARDA. A very handsome cut flower with a lovely scent; flowers in bright red, salmon, or pink. Grows to 30 inches. Good, long stems and excellent in arrangements. Summer bloom.

ECHINOPS EXALATUS (Globe thistle)   *top*

LIMONIUM LATIFOLIUM (Statice)   *center*

ANEMONE PULSATILLA (Prairie windflower)   *bottom*

IRIS KAEMPFERI *top*

ANEMONE HUPEHENSIS (Japanese anemone) *center*

GEUM CHILOSENSE *bottom*

D<small>ELPHINIUM</small> *top*

C<small>HRYSANTHEMUM</small> M<small>ORIFOLIUM</small>
   (Florist's chrysanthemum) *center*

D<small>IANTHUS</small> D<small>ELTOIDES</small> (Maiden pink) *bottom*

ACHILLEA PTARMICA (Yarrow)   *top*

ANEMONE CORONARIA (Poppy flowered anemone)   *center*

AQUILEGIA ALPINA (Dwarf columbine)   *bottom*

KNIPHOFIA *top*

RUDBECKIA HIRTA (Coneflower) *center*

IRIS CRISTATA *bottom*

CHRYSANTHEMUM COCCINEUM (Painted daisy) *top*

BEARDED IRIS *center*

DIANTHUS BARBATUS (Sweet William) *bottom*

HELIOPSIS (Orange sunflower)   *top*

MONARDA DIDYMA (Bee balm)   *center*

SCABIOSA CAUCASICA (Pincushion flower)   *bottom*

Hᴇᴍᴇʀᴏᴄᴀʟʟɪs (Daylily)   *top*

Hᴇʟᴇɴɪᴜᴍ (Helen's flower)   *center*

Pʀɪᴍᴜʟᴀ (Primrose summer phlox)   *bottom*

Phlox Paniculata (Summer phlox)   *top*

Chrysanthemum Maximum (Shasta daisy)   *center*

Viola Cornuta   *bottom*

ASTER *top*

COREOPSIS GRANDIFLORA *center*

CONVALLARIA MAJALIS (Lily of the valley) *bottom*

ORIENTAL POPPY (*Papaver orientale*). Poppies, with their dramatic, bold orange flowers, do not do well in regions of hot-weather starts. Thinning poppies early is absolutely necessary so that roots are well developed by the time hot weather starts. Poppies should have a foot of space between them.

PINKS (Dianthus). Popular flowers and many, many kinds. Easy to grow, these come in rose, purple, or white. They grow to about 12 inches and bloom in summer.

PRIMROSE (Primula). These make better cut flowers than most people think. Many varieties; come in red or yellow or white. Spring and summer blooming.

PYRETHRUM (Chrysanthemum coccineum). A favorite and beautiful mum-type flower in shades of pink or red. Grows to about 24 inches. Handsome; blooms in spring.

RED-HOT POKER (Tritoma). Tall plants (to 40 inches) with striking flamelike flowers usually reddish orange; some yellow varieties. Grows easily and blooms through summer to frost.

*ROSE (Rosa). The favorite cut flower and perhaps the most beautiful; many varieties and many colors. Some easy to grow and others somewhat difficult.

SPEEDWELL (Veronica). Handsome blue flowers make this desirable. Tall plants that grow to 40 inches. Different and appealing. Summer bloom.

STOKESIA. Lovely blue flowers make this one desirable in the garden and for cutting. Plant grows to 16 inches with fluffy, blue blooms in summer to frost.

SUMMER PHLOX, MOSS PINK (*Phlox subulata*). These 3- to 5-foot plants bear numerous large, pink flowers.

*SWEET PEA (*Lathyrus latifolius*). A vine that produces an abundance of pink flowers; better for cutting than most people think. Makes handsome old-fashioned bouquets.

TRANSVAAL DAISY (Gerbera). Superb cut flowers with strong stems; beautiful pastel colors usually pink or rose. Many varieties. Summer blooming.

YARROW (Achillea). In late summer and fall, the white flowers of achillea are handsome and make a good addition to summer bouquets. Plants grow to 20 inches. Bloom spring to frost.

Here are some special notes on perennials that are often overlooked as cut flowers but are certainly handsome and can be included in the garden:

Achillea ptarmica, known as yarrow, has airy white flowers, and blooms in summer and fall—a good late season flower. *Echinops exaltatus*, called globe thistle, has steel-blue flowers and is especially handsome and dramatic in arrangements. Geum, with its reddish orange flowers, is most desirable for its color. Stokesia, with fine, lavender-blue flowers, should not be ignored, and Veronicas, with so many varieties, offer flowers in colors of blue, pink, or white.

In Chapter 4 we gave you care of annuals and perennials. Here now is more information about popular flowers. If you grow just these ten types of flowers you will have a dazzling and useful cutting garden, perfect for all your wishes.

CHRYSANTHEMUMS

Chrysanthemums, perhaps the favorite cut flowers, are grown by the millions by enthusiastic gardeners. These flowers are so popular that professional growers have experimented with them for years, with the result that there are many types and varieties: anemone, spider, button, pompom, single, and spindle forms, ranging from delightful miniatures to gigantic, dinner-plate sizes, in a rainbow of colors. Chrysanthemums are flowers that can be grown in all parts of the country, and their blooms last well in arrangements; thus, they lend themselves well to decorative pieces.

Mums like a very loose soil (with lots of air spaces) and a neutral one, neither too acidic nor too alkaline. Add 3 cups of superphosphate to a 25-square-foot bed to get mums off to a good start. Feed plants heavily in summer and fall with a 20–10–10 plant food. (This is the strength I have always used, and it does very well.)

In hot weather, mums will take considerable water: almost every day, although if they have to they can take dryness. Plant prestarted plants or rooted cuttings in a shallow trench about 6 inches apart. When the plants are up—in about three weeks—start pinching about 1 inch of the top growth; this makes the plant send out new branches. In a few weeks prune the stems to two or three stems per plant. Pinching and pruning makes for double the flowers, but if you prefer not to pinch new growth, that is okay. Just remember that without pinching you will have only one flower per stem, whereas, with pinching and pruning, you will have more than one flower on each stem.

Mums generally grow tall, so be prepared to stake them (on commercial stakes); tie plants to stakes securely but not tightly. Ideal growing conditions for mums are 60° to 65°F at night, 70° to 75°F during the day.

ROSES

Show me a gardener who isn't a rose-grower, and I will show you someone who has missed a great deal, because roses are superb cutting flowers. They are terribly expensive if bought in a florist's shop, but if you raise your own, you can live like a Roman emperor, with delightful roses almost year-round.

Most people say roses are difficult to grow, but this is not true. Roses are no more trouble than orchids indoors, and we now know how easily orchids can be grown. The "secret" with roses is not to pamper them too much and to know which ones to grow. Some roses are, I admit, temperamental, but most of the lovely scented, old-fashioned types are really easy to grow—the good ramblers and damask types, for example.

Buy dormant, two-year-old plants that are ready to be planted. Roses need a fertile, slightly acid soil with a pH range between 5.5 and 6.5, but the actual structure and content of the soil are not as important as its drainage capacity and fertility. Roses require large quantities of water for maximum growth, and they simply will not thrive in soil that does not drain readily. To ensure good drainage in the rose beds, put in a 6-inch layer of crushed gravel in the bottom of the trench.

Prepare the soil with utmost care because the more attention you give to preparation, the less trouble there will be later. If the soil is sandy, improve its water-holding capacity with compost, peat moss, and other organic materials. If the soil is heavy, add sand and compost. The soil must be porous and somewhat rich. Dig the beds at least 20 inches deep; rose roots are long and need depth to grow well.

Feed roses every other watering during growing season. Pruning and trimming the plants depend on the specific varieties you grow. If roses are your passion, look at the many fine books that are available on the subject.

SNAPDRAGONS

Snapdragons are another easy plant you can grow in your cutting garden; they are colorful, keep a long time, and make fine cut flowers. There are several nice varieties, so choose carefully. Snapdragons like a loose garden soil that has some peat moss in it. Use 1 part peat to 3 parts soil. Space the plants about 4 inches apart, and water them when they are somewhat dry. The snapdragons do not tolerate over-watering, so be a bit miserly when watering (only in very warm weather can they take water in quantity). The plants generally do not respond to feeding too often, so feed them only every other watering, or about 4 times a month when plants are in active growth. I use a 20–10–10 plant food, which seems satisfactory.

Snapdragons can take shade, but really like plenty of sunlight and do best in cool temperatures; so get them started in late summer when cool weather is on the way or in very early spring before hot summer days.

You can pinch plants if you like, or let them grow naturally; either way there should be an ample crop. A pinched crop will yield fewer flowers but over a longer period of time; those plants not pinched give many flowers in a shorter time span. Do remove faded blossoms whether or not you pinch plants. Support plants with stakes, or they will get leggy and hard to handle. After cutting one crop it is sometimes possible to get a second crop from the same planting; this, of course, depends upon when you start the plants.

CHINA ASTERS

Asters are old-time favorites, profuse in bloom, and available in bright colors from white to deep violet, and usually easy to grow. Set your plants into a rich soil, but do not plant them deeply. Shallow planting is best, but do not let roots get exposed. Be sure soil for asters is well drained because the plants do not tolerate soggy soil. Soil must be loamy and drain readily.

No pinching is necessary with asters, and you can let them grow naturally. Asters require good moisture all through the growing season, and some feeding is okay, but not too much. Use 10–10–5 about four times a month. Space plants about 8 inches apart and see that they are in a sunny place.

Asters bloom for three to four weeks in the beginning, middle, and end of the growing season. Since asters are prone to fungus disease, it is a good idea to use a fungicide.

BACHELOR'S BUTTONS
(CORNFLOWERS)

These are those delightful, small flowers that brighten any arrangement with their pink, white, wine, yellow, or blue colors. The type most grown is *Centaurea cyanus*, which requires a well-drained soil; these plants will not respond well in a soggy situation. Bachelor's buttons also like all the sun they can get. Once they are growing, feed them ever so lightly with a 10–10–5 plant food only a few times during the growing season. Generally, these plants do not respond well to too much plant food. Space plants 6 inches apart. Water enough to keep the soil evenly moist but never soggy.

These annuals may take a little more time and care than others listed here, but they are fine flowers and not too plentiful at florist shops. They are not considered a good commercial crop as, say, roses and carnations are, but they are delightful in the cutting garden.

CALENDULAS
(POT MARIGOLDS)

Calendulas are very popular cut flowers and are especially good for the home garden because they are so easy to grow: Just set prestarts in the ground, or grow calendulas from seed. The plants need a rich soil and plenty of sun. Space the plants about 10 inches apart and water them freely unless the weather is unusually cloudy. Generally, the plants do best in an area of good air circulation because they like some breathing space. Pinch terminal shoots to encourage side branching. After flowering, plants can be cut back to 4 inches and they will flower again. The orange, cream, or gold flowers will bloom all summer.

DELPHINIUMS
(LARKSPUR)

Next to roses and chrysanthemums, you cannot find better cut flowers than the stately elegant delphiniums—what colors and what elegant blossoms! The hybrids are incredibly beautiful. Delphiniums are also called larkspur, but larkspur are annuals, whereas delphiniums are perennials. The plants prefer a cool climate, but newer varieties will adapt to warmer situations.

I grow my delphiniums in a raised bed of rich, but crumbly, well-draining soil with some superphosphate added to it, about 3 cups to a 25-square-foot plot. I start feeding the plants moderately when they are about 8 inches tall; I use a 20–20–10 plant food every third or fourth watering. I water the plants thoroughly and deeply three times a week, and this seems to be a good schedule. Of course, if you have frequent rains, curtail your watering schedule accordingly.

There are many varieties of delphiniums, but perhaps the Giant Pacific types are best known, and to me they are the most beautiful. Unsurpassed for striking blue colors (although the white and pink flowers are also attractive), delphiniums make any garden a showplace and any arrangement a stellar sight.

LUPINES

I have grown Russell hybrid lupines for several years, and they are outstanding plants, producing many spikes of stately, lovely flowers in pinks and blues for summer color. The plants are said to be finicky, but I have not found this to be so; they grow easily with a good, rich soil and plenty of water. My plants get about 4 to 5 hours of sun daily and do fine. I do not pinch or feed the lupines; they do so well on their own that I prefer to let them be. However, do be sure the plants are in an area of good air circulation—they may not respond in a tightly planted site.

I can recommend lupines to even the beginning gardener because they are so easy to grow.

SWEET PEAS

I think sweet peas deserve more popularity, and so I am including them here. This is personal whimsy, but to me sweet peas are excellent cut flowers. Unfortunately, sweet peas like a cool climate; so if your daytime temperatures go past the 80s, they are not a good bet. However, for areas where summers are moderate, sweet peas are fine plants.

Sweet peas are a vine, and vine they do; so be prepared to have suitable supports for them—either a trellis or a fence, and tying is necessary, or they become a tangled mess. The plants demand a good deal of water and biweekly feeding with 20–10–10 plant food. Sweet peas also need good air circulation and as much sun as they can get.

Although sweet peas require time and effort—tying and staking and abundant watering—they are well worth their care. The flowers, in soft colors of pink, lavender, and coral, are delightful in arrangements.

ZINNIAS

Zinnias are fast, sure-to-bloom crops for the home cutting garden. Give them some sun, frequent good watering, and an occasional feeding of 10–10–5, and you will have zinnias for show and glow. In fact, zinnias are so easy to grow in so many climates I cannot offer any secrets or tricks for blooming them. Simply put them in the ground and you will have flowers.

VARIETIES

Most cut flowers have been extensively hybridized; that is, the best have been mated with the best to produce exceptional flowers in either form or color or for ease of culture. Hybrids are given varietal names or are designated in plant catalogs by color or form—for example, China asters giants, cactus type, full-ball type, powderpuff types. Chrysanthemums are also listed in this manner. It would be impossible to suggest specific types; rather, select the color and the form you like and grow them. Most flower catalogs have descriptions and color photographs to help you make identification.

Where a specific species is desirable, the name is listed in italics, and you can order it by this name.

6

Bulbs

WE HAVE STRESSED that annuals and perennials are ideal cutting flowers, but bulbs should not be overlooked. Bulbs not only yield spectacular blooms, but they are easy to plant and care for: no weeding or pruning is necessary. You can plant bulbs like crocus and narcissus in the fall and get dramatic spring color; plant tulips and hyacinths in the late fall for summer color; or plant callas and gladiolus in the spring or summer for fall flowers. All of these are handsome cut flowers.

Many bulbs are winter hardy, which means that they can stay in the ground—they do not have to be replanted at the beginning of each season. As long as these bulbs have a resting period, they will perform for you each year. But even those bulbs that have to be replanted yearly do not demand much preparation or care.

PLANTING

Buy only top-quality bulbs, and buy only from reputable dealers or mail-order suppliers. You are buying an unseen product, so you must trust the dealer to give you healthy, robust bulbs that will bloom for years rather than tired bulbs that may come up blind (without flowers).

Basically, all bulbs need a moisture-retentive, but rapidly draining, rich soil. They do not grow as well in clay soil, and few thrive in sandy soil. Dig holes for bulbs very carefully; the holes should be round, with a concave bottom, rather than pointed (pointed holes create an air pocket below the bulb). Plant the bulb's growing side up; this side is usually the pointed end or the one showing growth. Plant to the bulb's specified depth, which means that the *top* of the bulb, not the bottom, is the indicated inches below the ground level. Firm the soil over the bulb; do not leave it loose. This is a common mistake many gardeners make.

Most bulbous plants can live off their own storehouse of food for some time, but they should not be neglected when they are in active growth. Water bulbs regularly from the time they start growing until after the flowers have faded. Then taper off watering. Dormant (resting) bulbs do not need any more water than natural conditions provide for

SCILLA   *top*

TIGRIDIA (Tiger flower)   *center*

LEUCOJUM (Snowflake)   *bottom*

them. (More about resting bulbs in the summer-flowering section.) You can fertilize spring-flowering bulbs once a season, which some growers recommend, but I do not do this. You should fertilize summer-blooming bulbs as soon as growth appears and again in the few weeks before they bloom. Use a balanced food with a low nitrogen content (e.g., 10–10–5).

Now that you know how to plant and rest bulbs, look at the lists of the most popular spring- and summer-blooming plants. Those marked with an asterisk (*) are more fully discussed at the end of the chapter.

SPRING-FLOWERING BULBS

Spring-blooming bulbs are the most popular with gardeners because they give early color and are easy to manage. These bulbs can be left in the ground all year, and so they are referred to as hardy bulbs. However, remember that some bulbs may be hardy in one climate but not in another. You can plant all spring bulbs from September until the ground freezes.

Note that after spring bulbs bloom, their foliage must ripen for several weeks. Do not cut off the leaves, or the bulb will not be able to regain the strength that went into its growing and blooming. If you object to the unsightly foliage, fold it over and put a rubber band around it to keep it neat.

SUMMER-FLOWERING BULBS

Generally, in most of the United States, summer-flowering bulbs must be dug up in the fall and stored over the winter months. They can be left in the ground only if the temperature does not drop below freezing. Plant most of these

SPRING-FLOWERING BULBS

BOTANICAL AND COMMON NAME	WHEN TO PLANT	DEPTH IN INCHES	SUN OR SHADE	REMARKS
Allium (flowering onion)	Fall	3	Sun	Prettier than you think as a cut flower
Crocus	Fall	3	Sun	Always dependable
Chinodoxa (glory of snow)	Fall	3	Sun	Do not disturb for several years
Convallaria majalis (lily of the valley)	Fall	2–3	Bright light or shade	Fine-scented flowers
Daffodil (jonquil, narcissus)	Fall	6	Sun	The name daffodil is used for all members; good cut flowers
Fritillaria	Fall	4	Shade	Over-looked but lovely
Galanthus (snowdrop)	Fall	3	Shade	Blooms while snow is on ground
Hyacinthus (hyacinth)	Fall	6–8	Sun	Protect from wind and mice
Leucojum (snowflake)	Fall	3	Shade	Flowers last a long time

BOTANICAL AND COMMON NAME	WHEN TO PLANT	DEPTH IN INCHES	SUN OR SHADE	REMARKS
Muscari (grape hyacinth)	Early fall	3	Sun	Easy to grow
Scilla	Fall	2	Sun or light shade	Once established, blooms indefinitely
*Tulipa (tulip)	Fall	10–12	Sun	Old-time favorites that make excellent cut flowers

bulbs outdoors only after all danger of frost is past. However, some bulbs, such as tuberous begonias and agapanthus, can be started indoors and then transplanted to the garden later.

When foliage dies down in fall, dig up summer bulbs and let them dry off in an airy place. If there is foliage, cut it off to about 5 inches. Remove all dirt from the bulbs and store the bulbs in a dry, cool place (50°F) in boxes of dry sand or peat, on open trays, or in brown paper bags. Cool basements, garages, closets, and attics are good storage spots.

MORE INFORMATION

The following information supplements data already given on certain bulbs in the lists. Here you will find general growing instructions on these more popular bulbs to help you understand their needs.

SUMMER-FLOWERING BULBS

BOTANICAL AND COMMON NAME	WHEN TO PLANT	DEPTH IN INCHES	SUN OR SHADE	REMARKS
Agapanthus (flower-of-the-Nile)	Spring	1	Sun	New dwarf varieties available
Alstroemeria	Spring	4	Sun	Good cut flowers
Caladium	Spring	4	Shade	Lovely foliage plants; many varieties
*Dahlia	Spring	3–4	Sun	Incredible color range
*Gladiolus (gladiola)	Early spring	6	Sun	Many colors available
*Iris	Spring	4	Sun or light shade	Numerous varieties
*Lilium (lily)	Spring/fall	3 times height of bulb	Sun	Many kinds; good in arrangements
Polianthes tuberosa (tuberose)	After danger of frost is past	1	Sun	Very pretty in arrangements
Sprekelia formosissima (jacobean lily)	Spring	3	Sun	Not hardy

BOTANICAL AND COMMON NAME	WHEN TO PLANT	DEPTH IN INCHES	SUN OR SHADE	REMARKS
Ranunculus	Spring	1	Sun	Lovely colorful flowers
Tigridia (tiger flower)	May	2–3	Sun	Beautiful cut flowers
Tritonia (montbretia)	May	2–3	Sun	Excellent vertical accent in arrangements
Zephyranthes (zephyr lily)	After danger of frost is past	1	Sun or light shade	Fine cut flowers that last a long time

GLADIOLAS

These are popular garden plants because they seem to grow in any soil without too much attention, but they do need sun. Plants grow quickly, are dependable, and bear flowers ten to twelve weeks after planting. There are tall varieties as well as charming small ones, both types in a wide selection of color. When freezing weather is over, plant the small bulbs (corms) 4 to 6 inches deep and about 6 inches apart in a well-cultivated, deep bed (at least 15 inches deep). Keep plants moist because they can take copious watering. When buds appear between the leaves, give bulbs a complete fertilizer. In fall, dig up and store the bulbs if you are in a cold climate; in mild climates the bulbs can remain in the ground. When the foliage turns brown, cut off the tops, and then dry the bulbs in an airy, shady place for a few

GLADIOLUS COLVILLEI   *top*

FRITILLARIA MELEAGRIS   *center*

ZEPHYRANTHES (Zephyr lily)   *bottom*

ALSTROEMERIA   *top*

TRITONIA   *center*

GALANTHUS (Snowdrop)   *bottom*

weeks. You will see new bulbs on top of the old, dried, withered ones. Store the new bulbs in paper sacks in a dark place at about 45°F to 50°F until planting time.

Here are some good species:

G. coviellei (baby gladiolus). White, pink, red, or lilac flowers. Loose spikes on 18-inch stems.

G. hybrida. This common garden-type gladiolus has a wide color range and many varieties.

G. primulinus. This tropical African species has yellow flowers.

G. trista. Small plants, with 2- to 3-inch yellow, purple-veined flowers.

LILIES

Lilies are synonymous with grace and beauty, and in recent years hybridists have introduced some stellar plants. Easy to grow, lilies may be left undisturbed for years while they increase in display. As soon as you get bulbs—and buy the best you can afford—plant them, whether it is spring or fall. Give them a rich, neutral soil, neither too acid nor too alkaline, that drains readily. Sun is necessary for a bountiful crop of flowers, and thorough soakings bring lilies to perfection. Plant lilies at a depth of 3 times the height of the bulb; use three to five bulbs to a group, with tall varieties in the rear and low-growers in the middle and front of a planting arrangement. Do not worry if the plants do not bloom profusely in the first year because they are actually at their best during the second and third years. Eventually the plants must be lifted and divided; do this about 4 weeks after they bloom, and then replant the bulbs the following season.

Exposure naturally weakens lilies. Before or during the blooming season, feed plants lightly with a 5–10–5 or similar type of commercial fertilizer, but do not overdo it. Lilies may have their pests and disease problems, but nothing drastic; just regularly spray or dust with an appropriate preventative. Of more concern are mice. They love the bulbs; so if rodents are prevalent in your area, place the bulbs with screening at bottom of planting holes to protect them or put them in pots.

There are several ways to increase lilies; the easiest is just to divide the established bulbs. Or use the scale method; that is, at replanting time remove four or five, outside, thick scales from old bulbs. Then put the scales in trenches about 4 inches deep and cover them with sand.

Here are some good lily species and hybrids:

EASTER LILY *(L. longifolium)*.The Easter lily has fragrant, trumpet-shaped flowers on short stems. Several varieties are available. Do not grow this bulb in severe winter climates.

GOLDBAND LILY *(L. auratum)*. Flowers are waxy white and fragrant, with spots and golden bands on each segment. Plants bloom in August or September.

MADONNA LILY *(L. candidum)*. This lily has beautiful white, fragrant blooms. Plants die after flowering, but they make new growth in the autumn.

AURELIAN HYBRIDS. These plants bloom in June and July. The colors range from white to yellow, with many orange shades. This hybrid grows 3 to 6 feet tall.

BELLINGHAM HYBRIDS. The flowers are yellow, orange, orange red, and spotted reddish brown and appear in June and July.

FIESTA HYBRIDS. This vigorous group of sun-loving lilies blooms in July, with nodding flowers of mahogany, amber, red, burgundy, or lemon yellow.

HARLEQUIN HYBRIDS. The flowers are wide open, in colors from ivory white to lilac, violet, and purple. Plants grow to 5 feet and bloom in July.

MARTAGON HYBRIDS. These hybrids have many flowers to a stem. The color range includes yellow, orange, lilac, tangerine, purple, and mahogany.

OLYMPIC HYBRIDS. The trumpet-shaped flowers are white, cream, yellow, or pink, shaded on the outside with greenish brown, and bloom in July and August. The plants grow 6 feet tall.

ORIENTAL HYBRIDS. The August and September flowers are mammoth, with segments in white or red, often banded with gold or red, and spotted deep red, and are sweetly scented.

TULIPS

If you think that tulips are anything like those of even a few years ago, you are in for a big surprise. There are many new varieties, and the tulip has climbed from an ordinary flower to an extraordinary one. There are parrot kinds, fringed ones, tall ones, small ones, cottage types, Darwin, Mendel, and so on. Some tulips are so utterly beautiful that they stagger the imagination.

Because there are so many types of tulips, select the ones that appeal to you—the small ones for a woodsy planting, the tall, regal type for borders. Do select both early- and late-blooming ones so that you can enjoy the flowers for many months rather than a few weeks. Give plants a sunny place where they are protected from strong winds. Use a light, well-drained soil; tulips will not grow in very sandy soil or clay soil.

It is generally best to plant the bulbs deep, 10 to 12 inches below the surface, say, because then there is less danger of fungus starting. Set early-flowering tulip bulbs 4 inches apart, Darwins about 6 inches apart. And if you are planting large areas of tulips, it is best to dig out the entire area; then insert bulbs and replace with soil rather than plant bulbs one at a time.

Plant bulbs in a prepared soil bed between October and the middle of November. They can be left in the ground or lifted; if lifted, annuals can be planted in the same space. In this case, lift bulbs with their roots and leaves, and then keep them in a shady place to ripen. When the foliage has turned brown, store the bulbs in a cool, dry place until planting time in the fall. Tulips need cold weather; in all-year temperate climate, you must buy precooled bulbs or store bulbs in the refrigerator for six weeks before planting them.

For simplicity, tulips can be classed as follows:

EARLY SINGLES. These old favorites are easy to grow.

EARLY DOUBLES. The flowers are wide open and long-lasting.

MENELS (mid-season). This type comes in lovely shapes and beautiful colors.

TRIUMPHS (mid-season). These are robust tulips, with a good range of colors.

DARWIN TULIPS (May flowering). The most popular type of tulip, globular in shape and of average size.

DARWIN HYBRIDS (mid-season). These giants have stiff stems.

LILY-SHAPED TULIPS. The plants have beautiful pointed petals.

COTTAGE TULIPS. The flowers are large and almost egg-shaped.

VARIEGATED COLOR TULIPS. These lovely tulips are quite dramatic.

PARROT TULIPS. The flowers are fringed and scalloped.

LATE DOUBLES. These are peony-type tulips.

FOSTERIANAS. The plants are dainty, and there are many unusual hybrids.

KAUFMANNIANAS. The flowers are large and early blooming.

DAHLIAS

These plants have tuberous roots and rest between seasons. The next year's flower is produced by the fleshy extension of the old stem. For best results, grow dahlias in a sandy soil and give them plenty of water and sun. Feed plants regularly with 10–10–5 and put a handful of bonemeal into the soil.

Plant early, but not so early that the plants will get chilled. Soak the tubers in water for one day before you plant them in 3- to 4-inch predug holes. Set the bulb in the ground horizontally. Insert a stake in the ground, beside the plant, because most dahlias need support. Keep the plants free of weeds. And when you water dahlias, really soak them.

As soon as the tops are killed by the first fall frosts, cut

DAHLIA   *top*

ALLIUM NEOPOLITANUM (Flowering onion)   *center*

CHINODOXA (Glory of the snow)   *bottom*

DAHLIA COLLERETTE *top*

AGAPANTHAS (Flower of the Nile) *center*

RANUNCULUS *bottom*

the plants back to about 4 inches above the crown, and then dig them up in a few days. Dry them in a well-ventilated place for a day; then store them in peat moss or vermiculite in a cool, but not freezing, area. In spring, divide the bulbs, allowing one eye or bud to each root, and replant.

Dahlias have been bred extensively. Before making selections, study all groups: giant formals, cactus types, sweetheart dahlias, dwarf ones, miniatures, the lovely pompoms, single-bedding types. The color range of the flowers is incredible.

IRISES

The bulbous irises are superior cut flowers, and their color and form are highly desirable in the garden. The most popular and frequently grown kinds are the Spanish, English, and Dutch types.

SPANISH IRIS (*I. xiphium*) have narrow and grassy leaves about 12 inches tall. The flower color is blue, but there are many shades available; all have the characteristic yellow blotch on the fall. Bloom-time starts in May and ends in early June. The plants need good drainage, full sun, and shelter from the wind.

ENGLISH IRIS (*I. xiphioides*) have larger leaves than Spanish iris, and the large, showy flowers are produced in several colors, with blue predominating. They bloom after the Spanish iris. English iris need a moist, acid soil and coolness; they do not respond in heat or drought.

DUTCH IRIS plants are hybrids, and although they resemble the Spanish type, they are more robust and floriferous. Flower color ranges from white to yellow to blue. Dutch hybrids need good drainage, sun, and a light type of soil. They put on their colorful display in March and April.

Plant the Spanish, English, and Dutch irises 4 inches deep and about 4 inches apart. In regions where freezing occurs, mulch over the plants in winter. After foliage ripens, plants can be dug up, dried, and stored in a cool place, or they can be left in the ground.

Iris reticulata is another lovely iris that blooms early in spring. Plant the bulbs in September or October, 4 to 6 inches apart, in a semishady location. The flowers resemble the Spanish and Dutch iris but are smaller; the plants rarely grow more than 6 inches tall.

Iris tingitana, known as the Wedgwood iris, is a beautiful blue color and grows to 20 inches. A lovely plant.

7

Growing

Flowers

from Seed

BESIDES GROWING FLOWERS from the prestarted annuals or perennials we discussed in Chapter 4, or from the bulbs covered in the preceding chapter, you can buy packaged seed and start your flowers indoors, transplanting the seed-lings to outdoors when the time is right; or you can start them outdoors. Besides being downright inexpensive, grow-ing flowers from seed is fun because you raise the plants from infancy to adulthood; you actually observe the complete birth and maturity of your blooming gems. And by growing seed you can plant any flower you want, rather than restrict yourself to plants your nursery might carry.

So welcome to the world of seed-sowing. It's a delightful world.

WHERE TO DO IT
INDOORS

First, if you are starting seed indoors, decide *where* you will keep the seeds. Sowing seed involves some care—watering often, watching plants carefully—so you should concentrate plants in a convenient area. The basement, kitchen, bathroom, window greenhouse, pantry, or any spacious room is ideal. Also, the appearance of growing seeds is somewhat bleak, so you want an area that others won't be looking at. By grouping the seeds in one spot that has a water supply and is private, you can avoid running around to water plants; and you can putter, experiment, and fuss to your heart's desire, rather like a writer who has to be alone to nurture his or her creation.

Note that a "spacious" room, as we refer to it, does not have to be a vast expanse of space. A room that is 5 or 6 feet wide and 2 or 3 feet long is fine. And the area should have constant temperatures. Thus, if your kitchen is cool while you are at work, but hot all night because you are a gourmet cook and have the oven and other appliances going for several hours, consider that unheated basement or pantry, where the temperature is fairly steady, varying only a few degrees. Also, seeds need some natural light (but not direct sunlight) or artificial light. (We shall talk about artificial light a little later in this chapter.)

WHAT TO DO IT IN

Once you decide where to grow seed, you have to decide *what* to grow them in: this means selecting a growing medium and the containers to hold the medium.

Your growing medium has to be sterile, milled sphagnum, vermiculite, perlite, peat moss and sand, or a mixture of equal parts of vermiculite, sphagnum, and perlite (all five mediums are sold at nurseries). Do not use a packaged soil-mix because it is too heavy for seed. Milled sphagnum has to be kept evenly moist. Vermiculite, or expanded mica, holds water for a long time. Vermiculite contains extra ingredients. Perlite, which is volcanic ash, floats and disturbs the seed bed if you use it alone, but if you mix it with a bit of sterilized soil (all packaged soil is sterilized), you will have a good starter. Perlite also retains moisture, which is what seeds need.

The containers for the growing medium have to be small enough to move but large enough to hold a minimum of ten to twenty seedlings. There are endless possibilities for containers: the wooden boxes (flats) nurseries use; the plastic trays, 4 inches deep, 16 inches wide, and 20 inches long, sold at suppliers; household containers like aluminum, frozen-roll cartons, milk cartons sliced lengthwise, one-pound coffee cans, bread pans, and plastic egg cartons; and plastic or terra cotta pots (an 8-inch pot will hold four or six seeds). Punch drainage holes in the bottom of the container if it does not have any.

HOW TO DO IT

You have the spot, you have the growing medium, and you have the containers. Now start! First, moisten the medium several hours before you are ready to start planting seed. Fill the containers with starter mix (vermiculite) to within ¼ inch of their tops. In a planting bed lower than ¼ inch, the medium does not get enough good ventilation. Next, open the seed packets and tap out the seeds into the palm of your hand. If the seeds are very fine (such as begonia and petunia) scatter them over the growing medium and then *very lightly* press them into the medium; actually imbed (cover with the medium) larger seeds like morning glory. Don't worry about spacing seeds; just make sure there is *some* space between the seeds.

Next, water the seeds. Here you have to be careful; just dumping in water will make the seeds float all over, and spraying with a mister will blow the seeds out of the medium. Water seeds from the bottom of the container, or use a watering can with a rose on its end. To water from the bottom, slowly submerge the containers into a sink of water, let them soak a while, and then lift the containers out of the water.

The most important part of growing seed is keeping them continuously moist. You do not want to overwater. Cover the container with a tent of clear plastic propped on four sticks to assure good humidity. Be sure the plastic does not touch the medium. Punch a few small holes in the plastic for ventilation, or else too *much* moisture will accumulate inside the tent. (Remove the plastic when leaves start showing.)

Once seeds are planted and the container is covered to retain moisture, give the containers bright but not sunny light. Keep the temperature at 75°F, which most flower seeds thrive on. Heating cables, sold at nurseries, will help keep the temperature constant. Put the cables at the bottom of the container before you put in the growing medium.

Even easier is to use a wooden container that has the heating cables attached. This can also be bought at your nursery.

Feed certain annual and perennial seeds with a very weak solution of half-strength Rapid Grow or Hyponex once every ten days until seedlings are ready for transplanting. However, most annual and perennial seeds will not need food. Transplant seedlings when they have at least four leaves.

ARTIFICIAL LIGHT

Artificial (fluorescent, incandescent) light helps produce healthy plants and speeds up the seed-germination process a bit. And you do not need a special grow lamp; any type of lamp, including daylight and warm white, is fine. Two 40-watt fluorescent lamps are okay, but a combination of lamps is better: two fluorescent lamps with four 8-watt incandescent lamps. Or try the new fluorescent/incandescent tube.

Lamps should be on twelve to sixteen hours a day, 6 to 8 inches from the containers. Because plants under artificial lights grow continuously, you will have to feed the plants with a weak solution of 10–10–5 plant food as soon as leaves appear. Again, keep the temperature constant and the medium always moist.

WINDOW GREENHOUSES

Window greenhouses are quite attractive and a rather novel way to grow seed. There are glass and wood, glass and metal, or one-piece, molded-acrylic greenhouses; if you want, make your own window greenhouse. Any window greenhouse, commercially made or homemade, fits into the existing window; you will not have to remove the window sash. A window greenhouse allows you to open or close the window when you want, so you can control ventilation. And inside the window greenhouse, humidity and temperature stay constant, which is the ideal way to start seeds. Use heating cables if your window greenhouse gets cold at night. You can put in an artificial light at the top of the window greenhouse, but remember that in window greenhouses seedlings usually get too much natural light; so you may have to block out very strong sunlight by applying a shade.

You have now started your flower seed, and if you followed all the "rules," the seeds will soon become seedlings, ready for transplanting outdoors.

HOW TO DO IT
OUTDOORS

Many annual and perennial seeds, such as nasturtiums, cosmos, and zinnias, are better started outdoors. If you do grow seed outside, first carefully prepare the soil as described in Chapter 4. Then plant seed in rows. By planting in rows you have space to walk between the plants, so you can tend them easily. The distance between rows of plants varies; check seed packets.

First moisten the soil; the shallow trenches between the rows should show signs of water. This indicates that you have watered enough. Label each row as to what you are growing. Even the experienced gardener is apt to forget what is where.

As with indoor seeds, keep the outdoor bed evenly moist. Remove weeds when they appear, or they will drain strength from the soil—strength your seeds need.

Thin seedlings when they are about 2 to 4 inches tall; this will give them more space as they continue to grow. To thin, pull up and throw away smaller seedlings or give them to friends for filling in various lawn or garden areas. Unfortunately, thinning plants always somewhat disturbs those left in the ground.

COLD FRAMES

If you have just, say, 3 × 3 feet of growing area outdoors, grow seed in a cold frame, which is basically a very low greenhouse, a glassed-in box set into the ground. In a cold frame you can maintain constant temperatures, as in the window greenhouse.

Commercially made cold frames, including the one-piece molded-acrylic bubbles, are sold at nurseries. But you can easily make your own cold frame from four posts, four boards, and a glass-paned window sash. Set posts into the ground, nail the boards to the posts, and put the sash on top of the boards. Pitch the sash slightly so water will roll off. Bury the posts about 6 inches; use 2 × 12 inch boards for the frame. It is a good idea to hinge the top so that you can periodically open it for ventilation.

To shade the cold frame, build a lattice over the frame or put the frame in a spot out of the sun. Start seed directly in the soil or start it indoors in containers and then put the containers in the frame.

Once your indoor seeds are up and thriving, you have to release the apron strings: you have to let your seedlings out. They need the roominess of the outdoors because now they are crowding each other as they grow and compete with each other for air and space. This is a most crucial stage because, once outside, seedlings have to be able to adapt to their surroundings; for this they need the right soil, the right light, and the right culture conditions. But don't be nervous—follow the step-by-step guide through the transplanting process and all should be well.

TRANSPLANTING

STEP 1

Transplanting young seedlings is actually a four-part process. First you have to transplant to individual containers, and then, after a while, you transplant to the outdoors.

When the first set of *true* leaves—four leaves—shows, you are ready for the first part of transplanting. In each individual container put a mixture of equal parts of soil, sand, and compost to ¼ inch from the top of the container. Lightly water the mixture. With a ladle or spoon handle make a slight indentation in the mixture in each container.

Take the ladle or spoon handle and gently, very gently, work the seedling out of its other container; try to get as much as possible of the root ball. Rough pulling of the seedling will shock the youngster and most likely kill it. Now put each seedling into each indentation, up to their collars. Firm the mixture in place, water it immediately, and put the containers in bright, but not sunny, light for about one week. This move gives seedlings time to recover from the first transplant.

STEP 2

Step 2 is caring for your individually potted seedlings. Before plants can go outdoors to the garden, they have to grow a bit and build up strength to fight the outside conditions of full sun, wind, and rain. This period of "training" is called *hardening off*. Protect the seedlings by putting them in a sheltered, *outside* area, like a porch or the back steps, for a few days and nights. Be sure the area is out of direct sun but in some bright light. After a few days, move the plants into stronger light and a more exposed area; keep them there for one or two weeks. On *very* cold nights move the seedlings into the house; the frost can kill baby plants.

While the seedlings are gearing up for their move to the outdoors, keep the growing medium moist all the time. If the top of the medium does not feel moist to the touch, water the mixture immediately. Gently and evenly mist tepid water over the surface of the medium. Also, lightly feed the fledglings with a mild plant food about once every five days.

Throughout this hardening-off stage watch the new plants for insects, disease, and legginess. If they are getting leggy (spindly), encourage branching and bushy and compact growth by pinching them back: nip off the top growth of the stem with your thumb and forefinger. This pinching is especially beneficial to single-stemmed plants.

STEP 3

About late April (in most areas) the weather has settled, and the seedlings have hardened off. Now you're ready for Step 3: the transplanting of the babies to the outdoors.

The first thing you have to do is condition the outdoor soil bed or the soil that will be in pots and planters. To be sure your youngsters survive, you must give them the proper nutrients. You should test the soil's pH first; that is, its acidity and alkalinity. A soil is neither too acid nor too alkaline if its pH is 7.0. Most plants prefer a neutral soil or one slightly below neutral (6.5 or more acid). Use an inexpensive soil-testing kit (sold by mail-order; see garden magazine ads) to see what your soil needs in terms of phosphorus, lime, nitrogen, and so forth. After testing the soil you should add some leaf mold, compost, or manure to the soil.

To get the bed ready, dig down with a spade or shovel 15 to 18 inches, turning over and pulverizing the soil until it is free of clods of soil. Rake over the bed so it is porous and mealy. Dig holes deep enough to hold each plant's root ball, and as wide as the plant's circumference.

Now *gently* remove each seedling from its container with a bread knife or trowel. Next, position each plant in the holes. Mound the soil around the plants' collars, smooth it down, and level it with your hands. Tamp down the soil firmly to eliminate air pockets, but not so hard that air and water cannot enter. Water plants thoroughly. Keep watering every third day, unless it rains.

STEP 4

Step 4 is the process of thinning out plants once they are thriving in the outdoor garden. Just as for seeds sowed directly outdoors, as discussed in the preceding chapter, thinning is really necessary to get the best out of your transplanted annuals and perennials: it gives the plants sufficient room to develop, and it helps prolong the season of bloom. Sometimes, thinning will require two efforts, depending upon the size of the plants. The space between plants should be from 2 to 4 inches for small plants, and from 10 to 12 inches for larger plants.

As you thin, remember to remove faded flowers so that seeding does not occur and to help prolong bloom. (Obviously, you will be doing this if you cut flowers.)

8

Reaping
the
Reward

LET US SAY you have followed half the suggestions in this book and have been fortunate: the crop is good. Now you have those handsome flowers and at little cost. It is time to reap the rewards and make colorful, attractive arrangements for your home. Your own cutting garden will give you hours and days of pleasure with your very own flowers. But it just will not do to cut the flowers and dump them into a vase of water. You must know how to cut flowers—there is a trick to it if you want them to last—

how to prepare them for arrangements—there is a trick to that too—and how to keep them living as long as possible.

It is wise to remember that a cut flower is still a living thing and, although taken from its mother plant, still needs nourishment and care. So let us see how to cut flowers, arrange them, and keep them indoors as long as possible.

CUTTING FLOWERS

At first you may think that a section on how to cut flowers is superfluous; but it is not, because flowers cannot be ripped from plants haphazardly nor can they be picked at any time. There is a time to cut flowers, just as there is a time to plant them. And different flowers require different handling techniques because plants have different types of stems: hairy, woody, hollow, and so on.

The main point to remember when cutting flowers is that, once cut, they still require water, and as quickly as possible. You can, if you have time, carry a jug of tepid water with you and plunge the flowers, after cutting, into the water, but this is usually a chore. Just cut and carry and get the flowers into the kitchen and into warm water as soon as possible. If you cut flowers and then leave them for even thirty minutes out of water, you are doing them an injustice.

It is best to avoid cutting flowers in the heat of the day (the old wives' tales about morning cutting is quite valid); cut the flowers in early morning or at dusk. In the early morning and evening the plants' stems are filled with water and in better condition to survive cutting.

As you go to cut flowers, carry with you a suitable basket or container to put the flowers in; it is messy to try and cut flowers with one hand and hold them in the other.

Be sure you have *sharp* knives or scissors because you want to make clean cuts, never ripping gashes. If you crush the capillary vessels in the stems, they cannot take up water later. Sterilize cutters occasionally to help prevent spreading bacteria to the flower stem and plant. I sterilize my cutters simply by running a match flame over them. You may prefer to be more professional and dunk them in a sterilizing solution, which is fine.

When you cut flowers, select those that are almost open; the buds should show flower color. Some asters, chrysanthemums, and zinnias can be cut more fully open than other flowers but, generally, cut when the bud is partially open and color is showing.

Always cut stems at a slant, for a simple reason: this exposes more of the stem surface to water. And always cut the stem below a node; cutting at midpoint can weaken the plant. Handle flowers gingerly: do not smash them around or treat them like a sack of potatoes. True, they can take some mishandling, but why stretch your luck? Flowers are fragile when cut, so handle them carefully.

When you get flowers cut and in water, soak them to their necks at room temperature for about two hours. Then move the flowers and container to an airy, cool (65°F) place, overnight if possible. In a cool spot at night, plants transpire little; thus, stems and leaves stay crisp and filled with water.

When you are ready to arrange your flowers, recut the stems. Plants with woody stems should be split (from the bottom, 6 to 8 inches), and you can smash these stems with a tap of a hammer. Immerse hairy-stemmed plants in tepid water. Recut hollow-stemmed flowers under water. (Plants with oozy stems should be seared with a match flame.)

Recutting stems under water may sound silly, but it does help preserve the quality of flowers like snapdragons, China asters, marguerites, sweet peas, and marigolds. What happens is that air bubbles can form during the brief period it takes to cut the flowers. The bubbles form because the crushed stems cannot take up moisture. If you slice off ¼ inch of the stem under water, it prevents a new air bubble from forming.

When flowers are arranged, strip all leaves below the water line, because foliage decomposes rapidly. Most flowers are not fussy about the quality of water, so regular tap water is fine. A few chips of charcoal will keep water sweet and odorless.

There are packaged, prepared chemicals that come with cut flowers from florist shops; use them if you like. Quite frankly, I have never seen any difference between flowers in plain water or flowers with chemicals added to the water —the flowers in either instance last the same time.

HINTS FOR CUTTING SPECIFIC FLOWERS

Through the years I have found that different flowers respond to different treatment; so here is a rundown on how to cut and handle some favorite flowers.

ASTER	Cut flowers when they are nearly open. Then place them in warm water. Recut stems under water. Flowers can last three weeks.
BABY'S BREATH	Cut sprays when they are nearly half-open. Soak flowers in cold water overnight. Lasts two weeks.

BACHELOR'S BUTTON Cut flowers when they are three-fourths open. Split stems in warm water. Condition overnight. Lasts two weeks.

CALENDULA Cut flowers when they are almost open. Condition overnight. Lasts two weeks.

CALLA LILY Cut at any stage. Submerge in cold water for a few hours and then remove. Cut stems again under water. Lasts two weeks.

CANDYTUFT Cut when flowers are half-open. Condition in cold water overnight. Lasts two weeks.

CARNATION Cut when flowers are almost open. Recut stems at a slant under water. Let stand in cold water for one hour or so before arranging in tepid water. Lasts over two weeks.

CHRYSANTHEMUM Cut when flowers are almost open. Place in warm water. Crush woody stem varieties, and condition overnight. Can be recut after about fourteen days and revitalized in warm water. Lasts two weeks.

CLARKIA Cut flowers when they are almost open. Crush stems, and let stand in cold water overnight. Lasts ten days.

DAHLIA	Cut flowers when they are fully open. Condition overnight in cool water. Lasts ten days.
DELPHINIUM	Cut when half-flower spike shows color. Condition overnight in cool water. Lasts about ten days.
DIANTHUS	Cut when flowers are half-open. Crush stems. Condition overnight in cool water. Lasts about a week.
FORGET-ME-NOT	Cut when flowers are half-open and immerse stems in warm water overnight. Recut and replace in warm water next day. Lasts five days.
GERBERA	Cut flowers when they are open. Soak flowers in cold water overnight. Lasts about a week.
LARKSPUR	Cut when spray is about one-fourth open. Place stems in water and condition overnight. Flowers last about one week.
MARGUERITE	Cut flowers when they are fully open. Recut stems under cold water. Lasts ten days.
MARIGOLD	Cut flowers when they are open. Recut stems and then place in cold water. Lasts about fourteen days.
ROSE	Cut when three-quarters open. Cut stems so that two leaf nodes remain on plant; cut just above this second node

or eye. Cut in late afternoon. Recut stem under a leaf node and split; then remove foliage from base of stem. Submerge stem in cold water overnight if possible.

SNAPDRAGON — Cut when flowers are half-open and condition in tepid water.

STOCK — Cut when flowers are almost fully open. Condition in cold water overnight if possible. Lasts about ten days.

TULIP — Cut when in full bud; make cut above white portion on the stem. Put stems in deep water up to buds. In four to six days recut stems, submerge again, and use. Lasts about a week.

WALLFLOWER — Cut when nearly open. Soak stems in cold water. Lasts about a week.

ZINNIA — Cut when flowers are almost completely open. Remove almost all leaves. Submerge in cold water for a few hours. Lasts about ten days.

KEEPING FLOWERS FRESH

Many times, after people cut flowers and put them in a vase of water, they forget them. Do *not* do this. Cut flowers, like any living plant, absorb water, and water evaporates. Thus, in one short sentence: Replenish water daily, and your flowers will last a long time. After several days you might want to recut stems to a shorter length and rearrange flowers; this will prolong the flowers' lives by several days. Finally, you can use the flowers one last time in another variation by floating them in water.

To keep flowers fresh, keep them out of drafts; they last significantly longer in a quiet place. If night temperatures are cool, flowers will also last longer than in a heated room. Also, it is best to keep flowers away from direct sunlight, which can wilt them.

FLOWER ARRANGING

Arranging flowers is an art in itself, and it is difficult to cover it in a short space; so here we only give the rudimentary elements of flower arranging. There are many books on flower arranging at libraries to help you.

You can learn a great deal about flower arranging by observing pictures and by really looking at the arrangements you see in florist shops. There are some basic rules of design: (1) Scale: the size of the flowers must relate to each other harmoniously; large, medium, and small flowers should be placed strategically to create a whole; (2) Balance: the arrangement should lean to neither left nor right but be in balance; this is achieved by repeating a flower several times in the total arrangement; (3) Proportion: this refers to the vertical and horizontal aspects of a bouquet; there should be proportion between the vertical and horizontal elements. Tall flowers should be balanced with a low mass of flowers.

In addition to the well-known vertical and horizontal arrangement, where the emphasis is either on height or mass (width), there are designs that use a cascading effect and some that are fashioned on the arc. These are considered the more artistic arrangements because they are simple (few flowers) but require strategy to arrange; the technique is derived from Japanese methods. The arc is a pleasing shape to the eye, and thus these arrangements are popular. There are also old-fashioned arrangements reminiscent of the English bouquets, where a great many flowers were used and a mass of color created.

The selection of color for an arrangement is also very important; colors must complement each other, and there should not be jarring effects such as blue flowers next to orange ones. Use orange/yellow/gold and red flowers for an arrangement or white and blue flowers. These are not rigid rules on flower color in arranging; what you use depends on what you like. I have seen appealing arrangements made with ten different colors, but in these cases the flowers were well placed for balance and harmony throughout.

When you are arranging flowers, always consider the container as part of the total piece. Generally, the simple glass container or vase is best for most flowers, and its size should be in keeping with the size of the arrangement. Two dozen flowers crammed into a tiny vase will not be pretty; they will just look crowded. Six flowers in a huge container will appear uncomplicated but the overall effect is incongruous to the eye.

To select the proper size container, keep in mind that the container should be half as tall as the arrangement itself and half as wide as the span of the flowers. There are always exceptions of course (a single tulip in a glass), but generally the above guidelines are feasible for most bouquets.

To anchor the arrangement in a vase, many people use frogs (wire or plastic receptacles) to hold the flowers in place. (Or you can use florist's clay.) Start by inserting flower stems in the center and work from left to right after you have a small grouping of blooms at the center.

In closing let me say that I have had my best successes with flowers by using either a great many of them in one arrangement, or very few.

9

Preserving Flowers

PRESERVING THE BEAUTY of flowers has been done for centuries in many ways; you yourself may have at one time put a flower into a book and pressed it. Years later, crinkled and brittle, the flower was still there. This is one form of drying flowers. Today there are several ways of drying flowers with chemicals; generally, silica gel, a modern material, is used, and it can preserve flowers beautifully—even their color.

Not to be confused with preserved flowers are the ever-lasting flowers. These flowers have heads composed of tiny flowers surrounded by *bracts*. After being dried out nat-urally, these tiny flower heads retain their form and color for many months. I have had statice that lasted over a year. There are several popular everlasting flowers which will be discussed at the end of this chapter.

DRIED AND PRESSED FLOWERS

Silica gel is a compound that looks like sand and has the capacity to absorb 40 percent of its weight in water. In the form used for drying flowers, the sandlike crystals are mixed with larger crystals that are blue when dry and pink when moist (coated with a nickle compound). These pink crystals warn the user that the gel itself has absorbed all the water it can, and before the silica gel can be used again it must be dried in a warm oven until the pink crystals turn blue again.

The procedure for drying flowers in silica gel is quite simple. Pour about 2 inches of silica gel into a shoebox or a tin cake-container. Place flower heads face up or ar-range sprays of flowers horizontally on the gel and add a thin layer of the compound to cover the flowers. Put a cover on the container and leave the container for a few days.

After several days, remove the cover and brush away the gel with a soft brush or shake the flower gently. The flower is now ready for arrangement; if the stems have been cut (and many people do cut the stems off), you can make ar-tificial ones from wire wrapped in green florist tape.

You can also dry flowers naturally; that is, hang them

upside down, tie the stems in bundles, and suspend the bundles from a wire or string in an attic ceiling, where it is dry and somewhat cool. Leave the flowers hanging for several days, until they are dried. These preserved flowers will not last as long as those done in silica gel, but they do last for some time.

Pressed flowers are still another reward of growing flowers. The best flowers for pressing are those that are flat, like daisies. To press flowers you need a large board, some white blotting paper, silica gel, a large plastic bag to hold the board, and some weights. Put a layer of blotting paper on the board and then cover it with a thin coating of silica gel. Now put the flowers on the gel—be sure the petals do not touch each other—and cover the flowers with gel. Next, put a layer of tissue paper, silica gel, and then blotting paper over the flowers so you have a sandwich. Place the board and flowers in the plastic bag and seal it. Put weights like books or bricks on top of the flowers. At the end of a week, remove the pressed blossoms and use them to decorate things like boxes or wall plaques.

POTPOURRIS

From ancient Egyptian times, right down through the ages, potpourris have been popular. Potpourris, which have been around for centuries, are pots or jars filled with fragrant flower petals and used to scent homes and closets. Indeed, walking into a room where there is a potpourri is a delightful experience.

There are several ways to make a potpourri, but here we look at two methods: moist and dry.

The moist method is something of a bother to use, but the

fragrance achieved is heavenly and long-lasting. Here is the basic procedure. Pick petals and then let them dry naturally (usually roses are used). When the petals are somewhat leathery (after about two days), they will be reduced in size about 50 percent. Now, put a layer of the dried petals in a crock or other watertight vessel. Fill the rest of the container two-thirds full, using 2 cups of flower petals to ¾ cup of salt. Cover, and store the vessel in a dry, shady place for about ten days. By that time the petals will be of a cakelike consistency. Break up the caked base and add it to other ingredients, such as spices and herbs. Seal and store the mixture for about six weeks, shaking and mixing now and then.

After six weeks, add the oils and seal and cure another few weeks. Then transfer the potpourri into decorative containers. Keep the containers closed at all times, except when they are being used.

Dry potpourris are easy to make and done with dried petals. First, dry the petals until they are crackly; this should take about ten days in a shady, cool place. Combine the petals with spices or herbs and mix well. Seal the mixture in a plastic bag for four to five weeks and give it a daily shaking. Then transfer the potpourri to decorative containers.

INGREDIENTS

Most potpourris are made of rose or lavender petals, but almost any scented flower can be used, including rose geraniums and lemon verbena. Herbs add body to the potpourri, and sometimes spices such as cloves, allspice, and nutmeg go into a potpourri. Gum benzoin or a vegetable such as orrisroot is often used as a fixative with the petals, herbs, and spices.

DRY POTPOURRIS

ROSE POTPOURRI

6 cups dried rose petals
3 cups dried rose leaves
½ cup orrisroot powder
⅙ cup ground cloves
2 drops oil of roses

Gently mix the dried materials, slowly but thoroughly. Add the oil of rose a drop at a time; mix in thoroughly. Seal the jar and cure in a dry, dark place for about a month; stir occasionally.

LAVENDER POTPOURRI

2 cups dried lavender flowers
1 tablespoon dried lemon peel
4 tablespoons orrisroot powder
2 tablespoons dried rosemary
5 drops oil of lavender
1 teaspoon benzoic acid powder

Put all ingredients in a jar and gently combine. Add the oil, a drop at a time; combine as you add it. Seal and store in a dark, dry place for about a month; shake occasionally.

MIXED-FLOWER POTPOURRI

1 cup dried zinnia petals
1 cup dried rose petals
1 teaspoon dried lemon peel
2 drops oil of potpourri

Gently combine all dried ingredients. Add the oil a drop at a time; mix well. Seal and cure for about a month in a dry, dark place. Shake the potpourri occasionally.

SACHETS

A sachet is generally a little bag of dried flower petals. It is placed in drawers to scent clothing or linens. Enclosed in fabric, the petals emit a heavy and intense aroma. The most common sachet is made of rose petals and rosemary, with cinnamon, clove, or nutmeg added as fixatives. Mix all dried parts together and pour the mixture into a small muslin or silk sack or bag.

Ingredients for potpourris and sachets are found at pharmacies and sometimes in health stores or through ads in garden and herb magazines.

RECIPES

ROSE SACHET

> 3 cups dried rosebuds
> 2 cups vetiver
> 4 tablespoons sandalwood

Mix all ingredients thoroughly and put into small, cotton sachet or similar type bags. Vetiver is rootlike in texture; pull apart and crush into small pieces before adding to rosebuds.

ROSE LAVENDER SACHET

> 2 tablespoons lavender petals
> 1 cup dried rose petals
> ¼ teaspoon dried orange peel
> 5 cloves (crushed)

Mix ingredients and put into sachet bags.

EVERLASTING FLOWERS

Everlasting flowers are the ones you cut and dry, and they stay beautiful for many months in arrangements. The drying is simple. Cut flowers before they are fully open, remove leaves, and hang, heads down, in an airy place. These plants are sometimes called strawflowers, and there are many of them that make flowers in the home an all-year delight.

Statice, or sea lavender, is perhaps the most popular everlasting plant. There are white-, yellow-, or blue-flowering types, and they are easily grown in the garden. *Statice bonduellii* is yellow, and *S. sinutata*, the most popular, is blue.

Another good everlasting is Helichrysum, which grows to 30 inches and comes in red, salmon, purple, or yellow. This, like statice, is extremely easy to grow in the garden and makes handsome indoor arrangements.

MONEYPLANT (*Lunaria*), an old-fashioned, easy-to-grow plant that has white seed pods, is sometimes seen in dried arrangements. Another favorite is globe thistle (Echinops). This is a tall perennial with handsome blue heads of flowers.

Other unusual everlastings you might want to try are:

XERANTHEMUM. Called the "immortal flower," it has papery heads of flowers; many colors.

Ammobium alastum. Very showy white flowers.

THISTLE (*Cirsium*). Rose red flowers; very pretty.

RHODANTHE. Rose pink flowers with silver petals.

GLOBE AMARANTH (*Gomphrena*). Beautiful; continuous-blooming annual; comes in many colors.

SELLING FLOWERS

I am often asked by gardeners if it is possible to grow flowers for profit—to make money. The answer is no. You may, if you like, try to do it, but the financial rewards will be small; this is confirmed by conversations I have had with people who tried this phase of gardening.

Today, with massive wholesale markets and suppliers, there is little demand for homegrown flowers. I suppose that if you have a surplus you could take them to florist shops yourself, but the expense involved in transportation and delivery, not to mention legalities such as licenses and selling off of your own property, would probably exceed the profits. If, however, you have a large acreage and want to try selling flowers to the trade, check with your local planning offices and secure necessary licenses and so forth.

Occasionally, I have heard of people successfully selling sachets and potpourri items to local plant shops and boutiques. There does seem to be some profit in this, since these items as of this writing are not mass-produced, and there has been a demand for them recently. This could be something you might want to pursue further, but again, you would have to obtain local licenses and a resale number from your state. Each state has individual regulations, so I cannot recommend any one route of action. The best way to start would be to contact your local city hall.

10

Food

from

Flowers

IF YOU HAVEN'T COOKED with flowers, give it a try; it is different, and some of the recipes, with flowers that you eat, are downright delicious. Chrysanthemum salad and chrysanthemum soup were my first introduction to flower cookery, and since I enjoyed these dishes I did more research and through the years came up with some of my own recipes. You can enjoy a variety of flowers in cooking, and we will give some recipes for a few dishes in this chapter.

You can also use flowers as a garnish for foods; this is an unusual and interesting way to make meals look pretty. In this case the flowers are not eaten but used, as parsley and watercress are often used (although these herbs can be eaten), as pretty accompaniments for the meal.

PREPARING FLOWERS

You cannot just eat any flowers; some are poisonous. You must know what you are picking before you use it in cooking. For this reason you will find our recipes include only the familiar flowers that most people recognize on sight.

Use flowers that are fully open. Sever the bottom crowns and wash all petals thoroughly in tepid water, rinse thoroughly, and then dry in paper towels as you would lettuce or any leafy vegetable.

Be sure that flowers you use have not been sprayed with any insecticides; true, most of the chemicals may be washed away but don't take chances. If you grow your own flowers, of course, there is no danger of chemicals. (Chapter 4 includes natural methods of insect prevention instead of poisonous ones.)

RECIPES

MARIGOLD RICE

1 cup brown or white rice
2 teaspoons chopped marigold petals

Prepare rice in standard manner. Add chopped marigolds and mix thoroughly. Serves 4. (Note: Marigold petals can also be used in salads, stews, breads, and cookies.)

OPEN-FACED NASTURTIUM SANDWICH

Cut up nasturtium leaves and mix them well with mayonnaise or cream cheese. Spread the mixture on thin slices of buttered toast. (Note: Nasturtium leaves contain ten times as much vitamin C as lettuce!)

NASTURTIUM VEGETABLE SOUP

Prepare a standard, homemade vegetable soup to serve 4 to 6. During the final 10 minutes of the soup's cooking, chop and add 3 teaspoons of nasturtium stems to the boiling soup.

CHRYSANTHEMUM CHICKEN

    1 frying chicken or broiler, quartered
    2 stalks celery, diced
    2 cups frozen orange juice concentrate
    Salt and pepper to taste
    2 small white chrysanthemum blossoms, chopped
    Garnish: whole chrysanthemum petals

Put chicken parts into a greased baking dish. Add celery and orange juice concentrate. Add salt and pepper to season. Sprinkle chrysanthemum on top of the chicken and bake uncovered for 40 minutes in a medium oven, turning once. Serve garnished with chrysanthemum petals. Serves 4.

CHRYSANTHEMUM SALAD

Toss together your favorite salad greens (to serve 4), and then add 2 chopped chrysanthemum blossoms. Season with oil and vinegar or sweet-sour dressing.

CAPERS

For years I've made my own capers from nasturtiums, saving a lot of money (especially when I cook veal piccante, which calls for capers). Capers are classified as either the bud of a Mediterranean shrub or the seed of the nasturtium. The difference in flavor between store-bought capers and homegrown nasturtiums is hard to distinguish. But the price isn't: it costs much, much less to grow your own capers from nasturtiums.

To start, put nasturtium seeds *on* a sandy soil. That's right, start them *on top of* the soil surface, perhaps in a pot holding one of your big plants. Add water and light—that's it.

After the plants mature and go to seed, gather the seeds (when they're green) and put them in the sun for a few days. Then steep them for a day or two in ice-cold vinegar with a dash of water. Now drain the seeds, peel them, and put them into fresh boiling vinegar for 10 minutes. Pour seeds and vinegar into clean jars. Cover and store the jars in a cold place for 6 months.

ROSE JAM

    1 orange
    1 lemon
    1 cup water
    2 cups sugar
    1 cup rose hips

Prepare as you would standard jams. Makes 1 pint.

ROSE CUSTARD

To your favorite custard recipe, add 1 cup of chopped rose petals. Mix well and chill.

FLOWERS AS GARNISH

We often see parsley or watercress used as a garnish for meals—to make the dish look attractive and to add color. You can create the same handsome effect using a few flowers—a few nasturtium flowers add beauty to any entree. A tiny orchid blossom makes a meal look pretty and inviting. Violet petals placed in flower form on a wedge of butter add a distinctive note to the meal. You can use flowers in many ways to make meals look attractive.

Garnishing the family dinner every night may be somewhat excessive but certainly, for those special occasions, a few flowers added to the dinner creates a cheerful ambience. And do use only a few flowers—no great bouquets on plates but just a touch of color.

QUICK-REFERENCE
TABLES

THE FOLLOWING LISTS give the botanical name of the flower (and its common name, if it has one) in the first column, followed by the height of the plant, its color, when it blooms, and how much light that specific plant requires.

The annuals and perennials listed can be grown in virtually all parts of the country, but, of course, planting times will vary with individual regions' climatic conditions. Further, if you buy prestarted plants, they will only be available in your area when it is time to plant them.

The following list of plants is by no means complete; it is a list of the flowers I have worked with through the years and found to be the most reliable and most useful of the many, many kinds of plants you can grow for bloom.

ANNUALS

BOTANICAL AND COMMON NAME	APPROX. HEIGHT IN INCHES	RANGE OF COLORS	PEAK BLOOM SEASON	SUN OR SHADE
NOTE: PD signifies planting distance				
Ageratum houstonianum (flossflower)	4–22 PD 12″	Blue, pink, white	Summer, fall	Sun or shade
Antirrhinum majus (snapdragon)	10–48 PD 10″– 18″	Large choice of colors	Late spring and fall; summer, where cool	Sun
Arctotis stoechadifolia grandis (African daisy)	16–24 PD 10″	Yellow, rust, pink, white	Early spring	Sun
Begonia semperflorens (wax begonia)	6–18 PD 6″–8″	White, pink, deep rose	All summer; perennial in temperate climate	Sun or shade
Browallia americana	12–24 PD 6″–9″	Violet, blue, white	Summer	Sun
Calendula officinalis (calendula or pot marigold)	12–24 PD 12″– 15″	Cream, yellow, orange, apricot	Winter, where mild; late spring elsewhere	Sun
Callistephus chinensis (aster or China aster)	12–36 PD 10″	Lavender blue, white, pink, rose, crimson	Late spring, where mild; late summer elsewhere	Sun

BOTANICAL AND COMMON NAME	APPROX. HEIGHT IN INCHES	RANGE OF COLORS	PEAK BLOOM SEASON	SUN OR SHADE
Centaurea cyanus (bachelor's button or cornflower)	12–30 PD 12″	Blue, pink, wine, white	Spring, where mild; summer elsewhere	Sun
Clarkia amoena (godetia) (farewell-to-spring)	18–30 PD 9″	Mostly mixed colors; white, pink, salmon, lavender	Late spring; summer, where cold	Sun or shade
Coreopsis grandiflora	24–36 PD 10″	Golden yellow	Summer	Sun
Coreopsis tinctoria (calliopsis)	8–30 PD 18″– 24″	Yellow, orange, maroon, and splashed bicolors	Late spring to summer; late summer, where cool	Sun
Cosmos bipinnatus (cosmos)	48–72 PD 12″– 15″	White, pink, lavender, rose, purple	Summer, fall	Sun
Delphinium ajacis (larkspur)	18–60 PD 9″	Blue, pink, lavender, rose, salmon, carmine, white	Late spring to early summer	Sun

BOTANICAL AND COMMON NAME	APPROX. HEIGHT IN INCHES	RANGE OF COLORS	PEAK BLOOM SEASON	SUN OR SHADE
Dimorphotheca sinuata (African daisy)	4–16 PD 9″	White, yellow, orange, salmon	Winter, where mild; summer elsewhere	Sun
Gaillardia pulchella (rose-ring Gaillardia)	12–24 PD 9″	Zoned patterns in warm shades; wine, maroon	All summer	Sun
Gomphrena globosa (globe amaranth)	9–36 PD 12″	White, crimson, violet, pink	All summer; heat-resistant	Sun
Gypsophila elegans (baby's breath)	12–30 PD 6″	White, rose, pink	Early summer to fall, but of short duration	Sun
Helichrysum bracteatum (strawflower)	24–48 PD 9″–12″	Mixed, warm shades; yellow, bronze, orange, pink, white	Late summer, fall	Sun
Impatiens balsamina (balsam)	8–30 PD 9″	White, pink, rose, red	Summer to fall	Light shade; sun, where cool
Kniphofia	24–72 PD 10″	Cream white, yellow, orange	Early summer	Sun

BOTANICAL AND COMMON NAME	APPROX. HEIGHT IN INCHES	RANGE OF COLORS	PEAK BLOOM SEASON	SUN OR SHADE
Lathyrus odoratus (sweet pea, winter flowering)	36–72 Climber PD 6″	Mixed or separate colors; all except yellow, orange, and green	Late winter, where mild. Not heat-resistant	Sun
Limonium sinuatum (statice)	18–30 PD 15″	Blue, rose, lavender, yellow, bicolors with white	Summer	Sun
Lobularia maritima (alyssum, sweet)	4–12 PD 12″	White, purple, lavender, rosy pink	Year-round, where mild; spring to fall elsewhere	Sun, light shade
Lupinus hartwegii (lupine, annual)	18–36 PD 12″– 18″	Blue, white	Early summer	Sun, light shade
Mathiola incana (stock)	12–36 PD 9″– 12″	White, cream, yellow, pink, rose, crimson red, purple	Winter, where mild; late spring elsewhere	Sun
Mirabilis jalapa (four-o'clock)	36–48 PD 12″	Red, yellow, pink, white; some with markings	All summer	Light shade or full sun

BOTANICAL AND COMMON NAME	APPROX. HEIGHT IN INCHES	RANGE OF COLORS	PEAK BLOOM SEASON	SUN OR SHADE
Molucella laevis (bells of Ireland)	18–30 PD 9″– 12″	Green, bell-like bracts resembling flowers	Summer	Sun
Myosotis sylvatica (forget-me-not)	6–12 PD 6″–9″	Blue with white eye	Spring, late fall	Light shade or dappled
Nemesia strumosa (nemesia)	10–18 PD 9″	All colors except green	Spring, where mild; early summer elsewhere	Sun
Nicotiana alata (flowering tobacco)	18–48 PD 12″	Greenish white, crimson, magenta	Summer	Light shade or sun
Nigella damascena (love-in-a-mist)	12–30 PD 9″	Blue, white, rose pink	Spring	Sun
Papaver rhoeas (Shirley poppy)	24–60 PD 12″	Red, pink, white, scarlet, salmon, bicolors	Late spring	Sun
Petunia hybrids	12–24 PD 6″– 12″	All colors except true blue, yellow, and orange	Summer and fall	Sun

BOTANICAL AND COMMON NAME	APPROX. HEIGHT IN INCHES	RANGE OF COLORS	PEAK BLOOM SEASON	SUN OR SHADE
Phlox drummondii (annual phlox)	6–18 PD 6″–9″	Numerous bicolors. All shades except blue, gold	Late spring to fall	Sun, light shade
Reseda odorata (mignonette)	8–18 PD 12″	Greenish brown clusters	Late spring	Sun
Salpiglossis sinuata (painted tongue)	18–36 PD 9″	Bizarre patterns of red, orange, yellow, pink, purple	Early summer	Sun, light shade
Scabiosa atropurpurea (pincushion flower)	24–36 PD 12″	Purple, blue, mahogany, white, rose	Summer	Sun
Tagetes erecta (hybrids and species) (African or American marigold)	10–48 PD 12″–18″	Mostly yellow, tangerine, and gold	Generally, all summer	Sun
Tagetes patula (hybrids and species) (French marigold)	6–18 PD 9″	Same as African types; also russet, mahogany, and bicolors	Early summer	Sun

BOTANICAL AND COMMON NAME	APPROX. HEIGHT IN INCHES	RANGE OF COLORS	PEAK BLOOM SEASON	SUN OR SHADE
Tagetes tenuifolia signata (signet marigold)	10–24 PD 9″– 12″	Yellow, orange	Generally, all summer	Sun
Tithonia rotundifolia (Mexican sunflower)	72–100 PD 30″	Orange	Summer	Sun
Tropaeolum majus (nasturtium)	12–18 PD 12″– 15″. Some spread vigorously	White, pink, crimson, orange, maroon, yellow	Spring and fall; summer, where cool	Sun or shade
Zinnia angustifolia (Mexican zinnia)	12–18 PD 6″–9″	Yellow, orange, white, maroon, mahogany	Summer	Sun
Zinnia elegans (small-flowered zinnia)	8–36 PD 9″	Red, orange, yellow, purple, lavender, pink, white	Summer	Sun

PERENNIALS

BOTANICAL AND COMMON NAME	APPROX. HEIGHT IN INCHES	RANGE OF COLORS	PEAK BLOOM SEASON	SUN OR SHADE
* Biennial † Many varieties				
Achillea ptarmica (yarrow)	To 18	White	Summer, fall	Sun
*Althaea rosea** (hollyhock)	60–108	Most colors, except true blue and green	Summer	Sun
Alyssum saxatile (alyssum) (basket of gold)	8–12	Golden-yellow, tinged with chartreuse	Early spring	Sun
Anchusa azurea (summer forget-me-not)	12–18	Pure, bright blue	Early summer	Sun or light shade
Anemone coronaria (poppy-flowered anemone)	To 18	Red, blue, white	Spring	Sun
Anemone hupehensis japonica † (Japanese anemone)	25–48	White, pink, rose	Fall	Sun or light shade
Anemone pulsatilla (prairie wind-flower) (pasque-flower)	9–15	Lavender to violet	Spring	Sun or light shade

BOTANICAL AND COMMON NAME	APPROX. HEIGHT IN INCHES	RANGE OF COLORS	PEAK BLOOM SEASON	SUN OR SHADE
Aquilegia alpina (dwarf columbine)	To 12	Blue	Early summer	Sun or light shade
Aster, dwarf type †	8–15	Red, blue, purple	Late summer	Sun
Aster frikartii	30–36	Blue, lavender	Summer, fall	Sun
Aster, English hardy † (Michaelmas daisy)	30–48	Blue, violet, pink, white	Fall	Sun
Astilbe japonica	24–30	White	Summer	Sun or bright light
Campanula persicifolia (peach-leafed bell-flower)	24–36	White, blue, pink	Summer	Sun
Chrysanthemum coccineum (Pyrethrum) (painted daisy)	24–36	White, pink, red	Early summer	Sun
Chrysanthemum maximum (Shasta daisy) †	24–48	White	Summer, fall	Sun or shade
Chrysanthemum morifolium (florists' chrysanthemum)	18–30	Most colors except blue	Late summer, fall	Sun
Delphinium elatum	60–72	Blue, purple	Summer	Sun

BOTANICAL AND COMMON NAME	APPROX. HEIGHT IN INCHES	RANGE OF COLORS	PEAK BLOOM SEASON	SUN OR SHADE
Dianthus barbatus * (sweet william)	10–30	White, pink, red; zoned and edged	Early summer	Sun or light shade
Dianthus deltoides † (maiden pink)	8–12	Rose, purple, white	Early summer	Sun
Dictamnus albus (gas plant)	36	White, pink, purple	Summer	Sun or light shade
Echinops exaltatus (globe thistle)	36–48	Steel blue	Late summer	Sun
Felicia amelloides (blue marguerite)	20–24	Blue	Spring, summer	Sun
Gaillardia aristata	20–24	Yellow or bicolor	Summer	Sun
Gaillardia grandiflora (blanketflower)	24–48	Yellow or bicolor	Summer, fall	Sun
Gazania hybrids †	10–12	Yellow and brown bicolors	Summer; fall; and spring, where mild	Sun
Geum chiloense (coccineum) (geum)	20–24	Yellow, red-orange	Early summer	Light shade
Gerbera	16–20	Scarlet, orange	Summer	Sun
Gypsophila paniculata † (baby's breath)	24–36	White	Early summer and summer	Sun

BOTANICAL AND COMMON NAME	APPROX. HEIGHT IN INCHES	RANGE OF COLORS	PEAK BLOOM SEASON	SUN OR SHADE
Helenium (various) (Helen's flower)	24–48	Orange, yellow, rusty shades	Summer, fall	Sun
Heliopsis (various) (orange sunflower)	36–48	Orange and yellow	Summer, fall	Sun
Lathyrus latifolia (sweet pea)	72–96	Rose, white	Summer, fall	Sun
Liatris pycnostachya (gayfeather)	60–72	Rose purple	Summer	Sun or light shade
Limonium latifolium (statice)	24–36	Blue, white, pink	Summer, fall	Sun
Lobelia cardinalis	24–36	Red	Late summer	Sun, light shade
Lupinus	48	Blue, purple	Summer	Sun
Monarda didyma (bee balm)	30–36	Scarlet, pink	Summer and fall	Sun, light shade
Oenothera (various) * (evening primrose)	20–72	Yellow, pink	Summer	Sun
Papaver orientale † (Oriental poppy)	24–48	Pink, white, scarlet, salmon, orange	Early summer	Sun
Phlox divaricata † (sweet william phlox)	10–12	Blue, white, pink, rose	Early spring	Sun or light shade

BOTANICAL AND COMMON NAME	APPROX. HEIGHT IN INCHES	RANGE OF COLORS	PEAK BLOOM SEASON	SUN OR SHADE
Phlox paniculata † (summer phlox)	36–60	Pink, purple, rose, white, orange, red	Late summer, fall	Sun
Phlox subulata	6–8	Red purple, violet-purple, pink, white	Summer	Sun
Primula (various) † (primrose)	10–14	Bicolors, blue, red, yellow, orange, pink	Late spring, summer	Sun or shade
Rosa (various types) †	20–60	A choice of colors	Summer, fall	Sun
Rudbeckia hirta (coneflower)	36–48	Yellow, pink, orange, white	Summer	Sun
Scabiosa caucasica (pincushion flower)	24–30	White, blue, purple	Summer, fall	Sun
Stokesia	24–28	Lavender blue	Summer, fall	Sun
Tritonia	16–20	White, pink, rose	Summer	Sun
Veronica (various) † (speedwell)	24–36	Blue, pink, white	Mid-summer	Light shade

BOTANICAL AND COMMON NAME	APPROX. HEIGHT IN INCHES	RANGE OF COLORS	PEAK BLOOM SEASON	SUN OR SHADE
Viola cornuta † (tufted viola)	6–8	Purple; newer varieties in many colors	Spring, fall	Light shade
Viola tricolor hortensis	10–12	Purple red, purple blue, white	Summer, fall	Light shade

Index